16 STONES ENDORSEMENTS

16 Stones is not a "look at what I did" book. It is not full of research about the top companies, nor mind-numbing "the survey says" statistics. *16 Stones* is the story of an ancient leader's amazing accomplishment told in terms that every 21st century leader will understand and can apply. —Norm Miller, Chairman of Interstate Batteries, Dallas, TX

16 Stones is powerful, a real home run. It will increase the success and enhance the life of any CEO or leader. These stones will enhance the lives and vitality of any team. This is a must-read for anyone who wants to be a successful leader. —Leon Drennan, Senior Executive (retired), Hospital Corporation of America

There are lots of books on leadership available in the marketplace today. However, you may be holding one of the most important you will ever read. In *16 Stones*, Dick Wells helps us understand what authentic leadership is all about through the personal journey of Nehemiah, one of the greatest leaders in the Old Testament; as well as his own very transparent journey of leadership both in the business world and faith community. —Rick White, Senior Pastor, The People's Church, Franklin, TN

While there are a number of books about Nehemiah, what Dick Wells has done is weave an interesting side story into the plot as he lays out the essential building blocks for living and working in today's environment. It doesn't matter what your role in life is; this book is a must-read. Dick's style is easy to read and under-stand. His book is one you will refer back to and share with friends. (I like to share my favorite books with friends, and sometimes they don't come back—you will want to have an extra copy of *16 Stones* to share or give away.) —Carl Roberts, President, Thinking Ahead, Nashville, TN

Wow! *16 Stones* is one of the best books I have ever read. It is at the top of the charts; I couldn't put it down. It was one of those books that I felt was written just for me. I've already started a couple projects/discussions that Dick's book inspired me to do. —Steven Dotson, President, Red Realty, Murfreesboro, TN

Dick has a rare ability to make the complex simple. His years of leadership experience give him insight on both the do's and don'ts of effective leadership. If you want a practical, step-by-step plan explained honestly from both Dick's successes and failures, then this book will give you the starting point—and the roadmap—to finish well. —Matt Austin, General Manager, KCBI, Dallas, TX

Excellent book; Dick has been able to capture the essence of current thought leaders, real-world business leaders, his own relevant and personal story, as well as the wisdom and power of God working through Nehemiah. A very thorough yet very personal approach. I will be using *16 Stones* in my university MBA Leadership course. —Dr. Ray Eldridge, Senior Associate Dean, Lipscomb University, Nashville

An outstanding job of connecting Nehemiah's amazing story to 16 leadership qualities so desperately needed in today's world. But it goes even further and connects those dots in ways we can all readily apply to our business, community, and family lives. I highly recommend it! —Ken Burrows, COO, Moore Colson, Atlanta

16 Stones is outstanding, and I have been very deliberate in reading a chapter (stone) at a time and absorbing the message. Dick's leadership insight is valuable, and to tie it so deliberately to an Old Testament character is wonderful. —Warren Smith, CEO, Cushman & Wakefield/Cornerstone, Nashville

Dick Wells has taken an essential story on leadership from the Bible and adapted it to the development of leadership skills in the 21st century. Written with clarity, direction and purpose. I believe this will be helpful in so many ways to business executives who have the passion and desire to succeed. Now that I have read *16 Stones* I know what I shall do. I will read it again. —Tom Hall, CEO, Premier Orthopaedics Group, Nashville

For more information about *16 Stones* and author
Dick Wells, visit www.16stonesbook.com.

16
STONES

Lead like Nehemiah!
Dick Wells

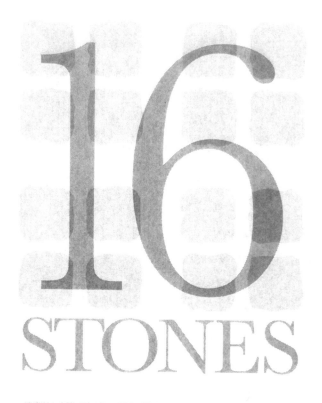

16 STONES

Raising the Level of Your
LEADERSHIP
ONE STONE AT A TIME

DICK WELLS

NEW VANTAGE
B O O K S

Published by New Vantage Books
An imprint of New Vantage Publishing Partners, Franklin, TN
info@NewVantagePartners.net

Design and typesetting by Jade Novak, Nashville, TN

ISBN: 978-0-9853038-3-9
Third Printing 2013
Printed in the United States of America

CONTENTS

DEDICATION

For Dottie: you have been the "wind beneath my wings"
for forty-five years. You are an amazing wife, mom, and Nana.
Thank you for sharing life with me. I love you.

For Elizabeth and Cathy: there is no greater joy than being
the daddy of little girls . . . and big girls.
I am proud of you both and love you very much.

⠿ ⠿ ⠿ ⠿

ACKNOWLEDGMENTS

My wife, Dottie, has read every word of *16 Stones* at least sixteen times. Without her help, advice, and encouragement, I would still be working on the introduction.

Ken Davis, Laura Flowers, Diane Lockhart, and Ed Smith all read and commented on the early chapters as I was getting started. Their input was valuable; their encouragement was invaluable. Thanks for giving me the impetus to keep writing.

Diane Cobb, Ron Keck, Carl Roberts, and Matt Shuff served as my "content editors." They labored through the whole first draft, gave me numerous suggestions that greatly improved the book, and told me to keep going. Thanks to all of you!

Every Thursday morning, 6:00 a.m. at Steak and Shake is "Matt Shuff time." Thanks, Matt, for hours of discussion we've had about *16 Stones* and a host of other leadership topics.

A special thank you to Carl who, back in 2009, kicked me in the rear and told me to start writing. Everyone needs a Carl Roberts in his life. Thanks, Carl, for being in mine.

My pastor, friend, and primary Bible teacher for thirty years has been Rick White. Most of what I know about Scripture I learned through his teaching. Thanks, Rick.

My only other pastor in the last thirty years has been Phil Wilson. I wish I were 5 percent as good as he thinks I am. Thanks, Phil, for being blind to all my faults.

As the book was nearing completion, I began to wonder, *What next?* Jeff and Nathan Sheets came to my rescue by forming Sixteen Stones LLC to handle the marketing and distribution. Without their help, I would have a thousand copies of *16 Stones* gathering dust in my garage.

By the way, Jeff puts up with me every Wednesday morning for an hour or so. We have solved most of the world's problems in our time together. Have you noticed?

David Shepherd and Greg Webster of New Vantage Publishing Partners, thanks for taking a chance on an unknown author. You have both challenged and encouraged me. Especially thanks for putting up with all my bellyaching about endnotes.

John Kleban was the most courageous and visionary leader I have ever followed. John taught me to raise the bar—for myself and for the organization. He saw a lot more in me than I did. He is missed.

Heartfelt thanks to Richard, Kurt, David, Julie, Mike, Murphey, Diane, "Boss" Watts, "Greenie," and Laura, who all faithfully stuck with me as I stumbled around trying to become an effective leader. We share a lot of great memories.

Early in my career, there were a lot of people who took a chance on me: Jim, John, Jan, Jack, Ted, Cliff, and Bob. When I was "wet behind the ears," they let me lead and didn't give up on me when I made mistakes—even big ones. Without their help, I would still be trying to make it as a very mediocre engineer.

Most of all, I want to acknowledge God, who knows me inside and out, but loves me anyway:

> For I am convinced that neither death nor life,
> neither angels nor demons, neither the present nor the future,
> nor any powers, neither height nor depth,
> nor anything else in all creation, will be able to separate us
> from the love of God that is in Christ Jesus our Lord.
>
> ROMANS 8:38–39 NIV

FOREWORD

Norm Miller

CHAIRMAN OF INTERSTATE BATTERIES

The shelves at Barnes and Noble are lined with books about leadership and managing, written by people who have either done it (Jack Welch) or studied it (Jim Collins). I have read many of the best sellers and they have been helpful, but the truth is—after 50 years in the business world—I am more than a bit skeptical when the "latest and greatest" comes off the printing press (yes, I still prefer to read with paper in hand) even though these books are often praised by the experts at the *Wall Street Journal* and on CNBC.

I read the prepublication edition of *16 Stones* as a favor to a friend. He assured me it was different and worth the investment of my time. He was right. *16 Stones* is not a "look at what I did" book. It is not full of research about the top companies, nor mind-numbing "the survey says" statistics. *16 Stones* is the story of an ancient leader's amazing accomplishment (Nehemiah rebuilding the walls of Jerusalem), told in terms that every twenty-first century leader will understand and can apply.

It doesn't matter what type of organization—business, church, college, or government—you are leading, or hope to lead, *16 Stones* needs to be in your leadership toolbox. Whether you are trying to rescue a floundering business, start and build a church, grab hold of a hot opportunity before someone else does, or replace Die Hard and Delco as the number one source of replacement batteries in America (that is what we did at Interstate Batteries), success or failure will hinge on how well you lead people, and that is what Nehemiah's story is all about—leading people.

When Nehemiah showed up in Jerusalem, the walls had been piles of rubble for more than 140 years. The people were dispirited and living in disgrace. They were surrounded by enemies and torn by dissension. They had no direction and no hope. Yet, only 52 days later, the walls were up, the people were united, and their enemies were thwarted. It may sound like a miracle, but it wasn't. The walls went up because Nehemiah—always honoring God and thereby having God's gracious hand on him—led, inspired, organized, encouraged and defended the people while they did the hard work of raising Jerusalem's walls (without cranes or bulldozers, by the way).

Though the events of Nehemiah's story happened 2,500 years ago, author Dick Wells tells the story in a creative and relevant way that is interesting and easy to read. More importantly, it is inspiring, practical and challenging, even life changing. In addition to relying on the thoughts of a host of leadership experts (Jim Collins, Bill Hybels, Max De Pree, John Maxwell, Peter Drucker, and Warren Bennis, to name a few), Wells spices up the story with personal anecdotes and snippets about Redd Fox (of *Sanford & Son* fame), *The Wizard of Oz*, Rosie the Riveter, Chef Emeril, and even John Wayne.

If you know you need to be challenged, then chapter 6 ("The Hardest Person to Lead Is Yourself") and chapter 12 ("Class Warfare") will get in your face and stomp on your toes a bit—they did mine. If you are discouraged and burned out, chapter 2 ("Soul on Fire") will ignite your passion to be a better leader. If you are frustrated because your buyers, salesmen and truck drivers seem to be at odds all the time, chapter 9 ("A Hard Hat for Everyone") will show you how to "get it done" with a team of people with vastly different skills and not much in common (wish I had known about Nehemiah 34 years ago when I first took the reins at Interstate). However, for some of you, the most important part—the life changing part—of *16 Stones* will be how the story ends:

" . . . to lead like Nehemiah, you must have a relationship with God . . . . and . . . He will put His gracious hand on you . . . ."

I know from my own life story that this is true. I have tried it both ways: living and working without God, and with God after I received Christ back in '74. Trust me, "with Him" is best. Without God, my personal life was a self-centered train wreck, and my work was crushingly hard and marked by fear of failure. With God through Christ, everything changed: my purpose, my values, my future, and my leadership. My personal life became one of joy and fulfillment; life at the office became (mostly) one of inner peace and confidence in God because His gracious hand is on us. It's not that I (we) haven't experienced difficult times, but just as God has promised, He is there with us to help us through the problems and sometimes He even carries us around them. My hope for you is that *16 Stones* really helps you *Raise the Level of Your Leadership One Stone at a Time,* and that you will discover how to live and work with *the gracious hand of God upon you.*

You are going to love this book—I did.

[Norm Miller has served as the Chairman of Interstate Batteries since 1978. Selling more than 17 million batteries per year, Interstate is the Number 1 replacement battery brand in North America.]

INTRODUCTION

If God has given you leadership ability,
take the responsibility seriously.

ROMANS 12:8 NLT

"Dick, they hate you."

"Who hates me?"

"The people who work for you."

That was how my boss opened a discussion about my performance after a few months in my first stint as a supervisor. I was flunking as a leader. My grade was an F. It was a lousy way to start that particular day, but it was one of the most important events of my life. It was the beginning of a journey— one I'm still on—of learning how to be an authentic and effective leader who people follow because they want to, not because they have to. Along the route I've made a lot of mistakes, learned from them (sometimes), and experienced more than my share of success. I couldn't have done it without raising the level of my leadership—a lot! I'm not yet at the level I want to be, but I'm still striving for it. In fact, I am . . .

SHOOTING FOR LEVEL 5

In his now-classic book *Good to Great*, Jim Collins identifies what he calls Level 5 leaders. They have the "personal humility" and "fierce resolve" needed to transform their companies from good to great. "Level 5 leaders," he says, "are a study in duality: modest and willful, humble and fearless."[1] About one of his Level 5 examples—Darwin Smith of Kimberly-Clark— Collins says he " . . . carried no airs of self-importance . . . never cultivated hero status or executive celebrity status."[2]

1

Two years after *Good to Great*, in a 2003 *Fortune* magazine article, Collins named Smith as one of "The Ten Greatest CEOs of All Time." Wow! Top ten of all time! What did all ten have in common according to Collins?

> If one thing defines these ten giants, it was their deep sense of connectedness to the organizations they ran. Unlike CEOs who see themselves principally as members of an executive elite—an increasingly mobile club whose members measure their pay and privileges against other CEOs . . . .Much depended on them, but it was never about them.[3]

Remember the phrase "it was never about them." Adopting it is one of the most important steps anyone can take in trying to become an authentic and effective leader.

Although Darwin Smith earned his way into the corner office of one of America's leading companies, in his heart he never left the Indiana farm where he grew up. According to Smith's wife, when he needed time to think through big issues and problems, his practice was to climb onto the backhoe at his farm and move rocks "from one pile to another."[4] Evidently he was a wall builder at heart, much like the subject of this book, Nehemiah.

Sandwiched in the Old Testament between Ezra and Esther is the story of my personal all-time favorite rock mover, Nehemiah. His story is a firsthand look at a true Level 5 leader who was called by God to tackle the incredibly difficult task of rebuilding the broken-down walls of Jerusalem. His critics (and there were many) said it couldn't be done: "What are those feeble Jews doing? Will they restore their wall? . . . Can they bring the stones back to life from those heaps of rubble—burned as they are?" (Nehemiah 4:2 NIV).

Against overwhelming odds (it would be 1,000 to 1 in Vegas today), Nehemiah inspired a discouraged and downtrodden group of Jews to accomplish the seemingly impossible. It wasn't easy. While building the wall, they had to defend themselves against fierce external enemies while split by internal dissension. Wall building was hard work in those days. There were no bulldozers, cranes, or backhoes to help. Halfway through the job they were exhausted and discouraged, but Nehemiah encouraged them to stay on task, and they did.

Like all leaders, Nehemiah was stung by criticism, slandered by rumors, and suffered betrayal in his inner circle. Overcoming these challenges with the *personal humility* (dependence on God) and *fierce resolve* (confidence in God) of a Level 5 leader, the job was completed in record time: "So on October 2 the wall was finished—just fifty-two days after we had begun" (Nehemiah 6:15 NLT). Just fifty-two days? A one-and-a-half-mile long wall constructed from a 142-year-old pile of rubble, using only their biceps and donkeys? No way! Why hasn't there been a movie about this?

Nehemiah didn't rebuild the walls just so the city of Jerusalem would have a handy place to hang decorations for its next big holiday. In the ancient world, a wall was essential to the security, significance, and success of the city. Without a wall, the city was exposed to attack by its enemies. It was a *"disgrace"* (Nehemiah 1:3 NIV, emphasis mine) and was bypassed by prosperity—the same thing that often happens to small US towns bypassed by interstates.

In Nehemiah's day, and still today, leaders have to do whatever is necessary to ensure the security, significance, and success of their city or company or church or whatever. For Nehemiah, it was rebuild the walls of Jerusalem. For you, it could be:

- Turn around a business that is spiraling down or stuck in a rut,
- Awaken a church that is dwindling and struggling financially,
- Make some needed radical changes in your family— or yourself,
- Grab hold of a new opportunity that demands a higher level of leadership from you, or
- Counter an unexpected challenge to your leadership from inside, or outside, your organization.

Whatever you are facing, your first task is to shore up your leadership. By raising the level of your leadership, your organization will become more secure, more significant, and more successful, now and into the future. It would be nice if you could become a Level 5 leader overnight, but you can't. You get there the same way you raise a wall . . .

ONE STONE AT A TIME

One of the best ways to raise the level of your leadership is by learning from other leaders—contemporary leaders like Darwin Smith and historic leaders like Nehemiah. If you had a chance to shadow Darwin Smith as he transformed Kimberly Clark into the world's leading paper goods company (look around your house for Huggies, Kleenex, Scott Towels), would you do it? If you could tag along with Bill Gates, Abraham Lincoln, Mother Teresa, or Winston Churchill, would you? Of course you would. What a privilege that would be. With Nehemiah, you get to do it because he recorded his leadership experiences in his memoirs—his personal journal that we know today as the Old Testament book of Nehemiah.

Nehemiah's Journal. *"These are the memoirs of Nehemiah . . . "* (Nehemiah 1:1 NLT, emphasis mine) is how the story of Nehemiah opens. It is Nehemiah's historical personal record, preserved in Scripture, of the wall-building project from beginning to end from his own point of view. Each chapter in *16 Stones* includes an excerpt from Nehemiah's memoirs exactly as he wrote it.

At this point you may be a bit skeptical, wondering, *Is a centuries-old story from the Bible relevant to twenty-first century leadership and worth the investment of my time?* The answer is a resounding "yes" because every challenge that Nehemiah encountered is one that leaders still face today:

- He had to mold a diverse group of people into a high performance team.
- He squared off against external enemies.
- He faced dissension in the ranks.
- He endured fatigue, burnout, and discouragement.
- He confronted criticism, rumors, and betrayal.
- He was tempted to become proud of success and to use it primarily for personal advantage.

Even if you don't normally turn to the Bible for leadership principles and practices, make an exception and stick with Nehemiah's story. You will find it thought-provoking, practical, relevant, and challenging. Don't miss this opportunity to raise the level of your leadership just because it was written 2,500 years ago.

Hanani's Journal. Each chapter in *16 Stones* begins with an excerpt from what I call Hanani's Journal. Hanani was one of Nehemiah's brothers—

the one who brought the bad news to Nehemiah that "The wall of Jerusalem is still rubble; the city gates are still cinders" (Nehemiah 1:3 *The Message*).

Hanani had a unique and close-up view of Nehemiah's leadership from the very beginning of the story to the end. His journal is my notion (fictional) of the story from the standpoint of one of Nehemiah's followers. For example, when the work on the wall first started, Hanani's Journal records that, like all good leaders, "Nehemiah spent the day walking around the wall, encouraging and thanking people, and asking them what they needed." Later, when the workers were faced with threats of attack and death, Hanani shares that Nehemiah "stayed on the wall, visible to everyone." He put himself in harm's way, just like the people who worked for him.

So the stage is set in each chapter from two points of view: Nehemiah's (as recorded in Scripture) and Hanani's (my conjectural view).

Leadership Stones. Each chapter ends with a leadership principle— sixteen in all—called a Leadership Stone. For example, the title of chapter 3 is "'Wait' Is a Four-Letter Word." The associated Leadership Stone is "Don't Jump the Gun, Don't Waste the Wait." Chapter 6, "The Hardest Person to Lead," is about the always difficult challenge of self-leadership. Its Leadership Stone is "Lead Yourself So You Will Be Fit to Lead Others."

The Leadership Stones are where the rubber meets the road. Applying them, or not, in your day-by-day leadership is what will determine if *16 Stones* is just an interesting read or a book that actually makes a difference in the security, significance, and success of your organization and its people.

"EVERYONE WINS WHEN A LEADER GETS BETTER"

Bill Hybels used that phrase to open, and later close, the two-day 2012 Global Leadership Summit.[5] Since "everyone wins when a leader gets better," that makes raising the level of your leadership important. It's important, but not easy.

There was no easy way—no shortcut—for Nehemiah to raise the walls of Jerusalem. It had to be done *one stone at a time*. And there is no easy way for you to raise the level of your leadership. It takes place one Leadership Stone at a time. But is it worth the effort? Yes, because "everyone wins" means you win, your organization wins, and your followers win. "Everyone wins" because if you change the way you lead, your followers will change the way they follow. Leading won't seem nearly as hard as it used to be, and together you'll accomplish more than you ever thought possible—even things your critics say can't be done.

The sole purpose of *16 Stones* is to help you raise the level of your leadership. Nehemiah's story will inspire you to do exactly that.

So if you're ready, the best way to start is to reach down and pick up that first stone.

THE CENTER OF THE UNIVERSE

Throughout the many centuries of exile,
Jews have always lived on two planes—the one into which
they were thrown by the accidents of history,
and the other, Jerusalem, considered by the sages as
the center of the universe, to which they were drawn
by longing and faith. (emphasis mine)[6]
AVRAHAM HOLTZ, *THE HOLY CITY*

HANANI'S JOURNAL

This is a disgrace. I'm ashamed to be a Jew. Everywhere I look there's nothing but rat-infested rubble overgrown with thorn-covered vines. Rock piles and half-burned timbers are all that remain of the walls. The city is wide open to jackals (both the animal and the human kind). No one goes out after dark. By sundown Jerusalem looks more like a ghost town than the great City of David. And it's been this way for 142 years! Will it ever change? No one seems to care enough to do anything, or maybe they're just afraid.

Eliashib brushed me off when I talked to him about it. Some high priest he is. "Too busy; not my concern; talk to the city officials," he told me. So I did. Our "grand" leaders, Rephaiah and Shallum, wouldn't even discuss it with me. They cut me off with the typical party line, "The king has forbidden any rebuilding of the wall, so there's no point in even talking about it. Do you want us to get our heads chopped off?"

The Jews outside the city in Mizpah and Gibeon are no help either. They're so preoccupied with surviving day to day, all they can do is scratch out a living by raising a few measly sheep and goats. I guess I don't really blame them. They hardly ever come to town and don't stay long when they do. On top of that, Sanballat watches every move they make and has threatened reprisals if they do anything that challenges his power.

I sure feel hopeless. Jerusalem is supposed to be our highest joy, but right now it's more like our lowest shame. I'm not looking forward to telling my brother, Nehemiah, about this sorry state of affairs. He's 900 miles away working for the king. I haven't seen him since we were boys, so next week I start the long, hot, dry trek across the desert to Susa to visit him. The trip will be miserable, but maybe Nehemiah can raise my spirits. He may even know how to pull some royal strings to help us out. Whatever. It sure will be good to see my brother again.

NEHEMIAH'S JOURNAL

"The words of Nehemiah son of Hacaliah: In the month of Kislev in the twentieth year, while I was in the citadel of Susa, Hanani, one of my brothers, came from Judah with some other men, and I questioned them about the Jewish remnant that survived the exile, and also about Jerusalem." (Nehemiah 1:1–2 NIV)

:: :: :: ::

JERUSALEM'S 9/11

In real time, as it happened, we saw the twin towers fall and watched the Pentagon burn. We saw the scattered wreckage of an airplane in a remote Pennsylvania field. We wept . . . we prayed . . . we gave . . . we attended memorial services all across America. We flew flags on our cars and put yellow ribbons on our trees. We vowed revenge and sent our sons and daughters to fight in the dust and heat of faraway deserts—places most Americans cannot find on a map. In an address to the U. N. General Assembly on November 11, 2001, President George W. Bush promised that we would never forget:

> **Time is passing. Yet, for the United States of America, there will be no forgetting September the 11th. We will remember every rescuer**

who died in honor. We will remember every family that lives in grief.
We will remember the fire and ash, the last phone calls, the funerals of the children.

But the truth is, as time has passed—less than one generation removed—
the wound to our national psyche has largely healed, and the scar fades
with each passing year. The Pentagon is repaired. Memorials now stand at
Ground Zero and in the Pennsylvania field. We still remember (there were
tenth anniversary memorial services on 9/11/2011), but except for those who
lost a loved one in the attacks or in the fighting since, life in America has
returned to the pre-9/11 norm. When we fly, we have to take off our shoes
and walk through body-scan machines. Otherwise, we go to work, raise our
children, mow the grass, go boating or play golf on Saturday, finish off the
week by sleeping late or attending church on Sunday morning, then cheer
for our favorite team on Sunday afternoon.

The events of 9/11 are part of our history, and like the assassination of
President Kennedy, we remember exactly where we were and what we were
doing when it happened (I was leaving the dentist's office). But we are not
obsessed with it. Like you, I mourned and was saddened when the twin towers
fell. I grieved over the losses in Pennsylvania and at the Pentagon. Overall,
though, my life today is little affected because none of these places were the
center of my universe. Not so with the Jews and Jerusalem.

The Jewish people have experienced many 9/11s and have been scattered into exile over and over. Yet through it all, Jerusalem has remained the
center of their universe:

Without Jerusalem, the Jews are a . . . scattered people with no live
link to the past and only fragile hopes for the future.[7]—Lisa Katz

The view of Jerusalem is the history of the world; it is more, it is the
history of earth and of heaven.[8] —Benjamin Disraeli

L'SHANA HABA'A B'YERUSHALAYIM

The very identity of the Jewish people is tied to Jerusalem. Without
it, they have no past and no future. From the time King David established
Jerusalem as the Jews' political and spiritual center around 1000 BC, Jerusalem
has been the *heart home* of the Jewish people. Their longing for Jerusalem
plays out in many ways:

- The *mizrah* wall of a Jewish home indicates the direction of Jerusalem toward which Jews pray.
- At Jewish gatherings, the shattering of a glass is a reminder of the shattering of Jerusalem.
- A small bag of soil from Jerusalem is sometimes placed in the grave when burial in Jerusalem is not possible.
- The final words of the Passover Seder and Yom Kippur celebrations are *"L'Shana Haba'a B'yerushalayim"*: "Next year in Jerusalem!"

The first Jewish 9/11 occurred in 587 BC when the Babylonians destroyed—*completely* destroyed—the city of Jerusalem. They leveled the walls, burned the gates, and smashed the temple to pieces:

> On the seventh day of the fifth month, in the nineteenth year of Nebuchadnezzar king of Babylon, Nebuzaradan commander of the imperial guard, an official of the king of Babylon, came to Jerusalem. He set fire to the temple of the LORD, the royal palace and all the houses of Jerusalem. Every important building he burned down . . . . broke down the walls around Jerusalem . . . . (2 Kings 25:8–10 NIV)

(Appendix 1 provides an overview of the history of Jerusalem up to the time of Nehemiah.)

To ensure the city and walls were not rebuilt, many of the people, including all the leaders, were hauled away to serve as slaves back in Babylon:

> Nebuzaradan the commander of the guard carried into exile the people who remained in the city, along with the rest of the populace and those who had gone over to the king of Babylon. But the commander left behind some of the poorest people of the land to work the vineyards and fields. (2 Kings 25:11–12 NIV)

About fifty years later, the Persians conquered the Babylonians, and a new monarch, King Cyrus, allowed some of the captive Jews to return to Jerusalem to rebuild the temple. For generations, though, the walls remained scattered, overgrown heaps of rubble, and the gates were stacks of charred beams and ashes. So a remnant of the Jews was back in the region of Jerusalem, a few actually living in the city, and they did not forget:

> If I forget you, O Jerusalem, may my right hand forget its skill. May
> my tongue cling to the roof of my mouth if I do not remember you,
> if I do not consider Jerusalem my highest joy. (Psalm 137:5–6 NIV)

They knew Jerusalem could not truly be their *highest joy* unless it was fully restored.

Though Nehemiah lived in faraway Susa, his roots and heart, like those of all Jews, remained in Jerusalem. It was home, not because he had lived there, but because his heart was there and Jerusalem was the center of his universe, his highest joy. So it is no wonder that when he heard that the walls of Jerusalem were broken down and the gates burned, the warm bed of embers for Jerusalem that reside in every Jewish heart erupted into a raging fire. He was willing to take great risk and give up his comfortable life in Susa to do something about it. In restoring the true center of his universe to greatness, he found what all Level 5 leaders must have: a purpose for their lives greater than their own self-interests.

Leadership STONE **1** A PURPOSE GREATER THAN SELF

Recall Jim Collins's observation about the top ten CEOs of all time: "Much depended on them, but it was never about them." For great leaders, it was and is never about *them*. Why would Nehemiah give up his comfortable life in the palace for the punishing task of building a city wall? Because his purpose was greater than self; it was to honor God and rebuild the walls of the center of the universe of the Jewish people.

To make sure your focus is on a Purpose Greater than Self, reflect honestly on the questions below.

- What—*really*—is the center of your universe?
- Is it self?
- Making the *Forbes* list of great leaders?
- Becoming a regular guest on CNBC?
- Owning houses in Manhattan, the Hamptons, and Palm Beach?
- Playing scratch golf?

You will never make it to Level 5 if these are the things that drive you. If you're preoccupied with "self things" like these, look around for a pile of rubble that needs to be restored—your business, your church, your family. Ruins cannot be rebuilt without courage, risk-taking, and personal sacrifice—*your* courage, *your* risk-taking, and *your* personal sacrifice.

Your first step in raising the level of your leadership is to spend some time identifying a Purpose Greater than Self. It's the first Leadership Stone you need to put in place—the foundation for everything that follows. ■

2

SOUL ON FIRE

The most powerful weapon on earth is the human soul on fire.[9]

FIELD MARSHAL FERDINAND FOCH

What a relief when we finally saw Susa on the horizon. Nearly five months of desert! What a trip! Nothing but wind, sand, goat jerky for dinner, and tepid water. I could hardly wait for a bath and a glass of wine. But the closer we got, the more I realized I could hardly wait to see Nehemiah. It had been too long since we last saw each other. I knew he had some sort of big-shot job in the palace, but until I actually saw him, I had no idea how BIG. He had it made.

We entered the city, found a place to leave the camels, then headed for the palace. We expected problems getting in to see Nehemiah. We knew that the palace security would be tight since King Artaxerxes had become king only because his father had been murdered by the commander of the royal bodyguard. How ironic is that! Anyway, after "forever," the head of security assigned an escort to take us to Nehemiah's private chambers. Wow! I have never seen a set-up like that! What a sweet deal he has. He's the king's cupbearer. He gets to spend all day sipping wine, planning and tasting the king's meals so no one poisons "His Majesty." As part of the king's inner circle, he monitors all the chatter, gossip, and intrigue of the court. Veeerrrrry cushy. Sure beats the hard-scrabble life we have back in Judah.

Once they accepted my story that I'm Nehemiah's brother, servants swarmed us. Some waved fans to cool us off, others washed our feet, and about a dozen or so kept running in and out with all the wine, dates, melons, grapes, lamb kebobs, and grilled quail we could eat. Can you say, "We were stuffed"?

It took a while for Nehemiah to get free from his responsibilities so he could spend time with us. While we were waiting, I began to wonder if he would care at all about the sad state of affairs back home. Why would he give up an incredible life like this? After all, if he gets crosswise with the king over trying to fix things in Jerusalem, he might be risking more than his job as the cupbearer. He could be risking his head.

NEHEMIAH'S JOURNAL

"They said to me, 'Those who survived the exile and are back in the province are in great trouble and disgrace. The wall of Jerusalem is broken down, and its gates have been burned with fire.' When I heard these things, I sat down and wept. For some days I mourned and fasted and prayed before the God of heaven." (Nehemiah 1:3–4 NIV)

PASSION TO LEAD

In describing conditions in Jerusalem, Hanani used words that stir emotions: "survived . . . exile . . . great trouble . . . disgrace . . . broken down . . . burned with fire." Nehemiah's response was to weep, mourn, fast, and pray—for days! His soul was set on fire, but it was more than emotion burning within him. It was passion.

Unlike emotion, which can be here today and gone tomorrow, and unlike sentiment or nostalgia, which invoke warm fuzzies and not much else, passion creates dissatisfaction with the status quo and fuels an enduring desire to do something. Passion will not rest easy; passion must *act*. Passion is essential for effective leadership. Why? Because leaders are defined by what they do, not by who they are. Passion will lead to doing! Management expert E. M. Forster makes the point clear: "One person with passion is better than forty people merely interested."[10]

Now, before you get too upset, I'm not saying that *who you are* (personality, character, etc.) is unimportant. It *is* important—*very* important. Who you are has a lot to do with your *potential* to lead. However, potential to do something and actually doing it are not the same. Integrity is essential for leaders, but people will not follow you just because you are honest. If you are a visionary, that's great. But people will not follow you just because you dream great dreams. There are a lot of honest visionaries who never accomplish their dreams because they fail at the task of leading.

Nehemiah had all the character traits that followers look for (integrity, humility, etc.). He had the potential to lead. But he had more than just potential. He also knew *how* to lead. His story is about actually rebuilding the walls.

I know this may sound harsh, but there aren't any books written—in Scripture or literature—about men and women who accomplished little or nothing, no matter how honest they were or how great their vision was. So, I'll say it clearly: leaders are defined by what they *do*, and passion is essential for action, for doing.

It is not your position—CEO, manager, owner, senior pastor—that makes you a leader. What makes you a leader is that people choose to follow you on a journey of change. Before they'll voluntarily go with you, though, one of the main things they look for is your passion for the journey. They want to know that you really care and that the fire in your soul will endure when the journey together gets tough (because at some point it *will get tough*, or tiresome, or scary). They want to know their leader's flame will keep burning even when drenched by discouragement, delayed by detours, or set back by defeats. Nehemiah encountered all these things, yet his passion burned hot throughout.

So if you want to lead, you'll need passion for leading, or you'll burn out before reaching the finish line. In *The 21 Indispensable Qualities of a Leader*, John Maxwell puts it this way: "A great leader's courage to fulfill his vision comes from passion, not position."[11]

In addition to courage, passion is also the wellspring of sacrifice, perseverance, and risk-taking. Did Nehemiah have enough passion to give up his cushy job in the king's palace? Would he persevere when opposition raised its ugly head? Would he keep at the task even when it was dangerous and risky?

Leading is not easy. It wasn't easy for Nehemiah. It isn't easy for you or me. But without passion, leading becomes downright impossible.

FIVE DIMENSIONS OF PASSION

Passion is essential if you want people to follow you on the difficult journey of change. When a leader has passion that will attract followers, what does it look like?

#1—Passion for the mission. The mission—purpose—of the organization is, quite simply, *the reason the organization exists in the first place.* As Jim Collins and Jerry Porras, authors of *Built to Last*, say of mission, "This is who we are; this is what we stand for; this is what we're all about."[12] It is a clearly defined purpose that people can embrace and have passion for.

You can *work for* an organization without passion for the mission, but you cannot *lead it* without passion for the mission. If you are there just going through the motions to draw a paycheck, the people who follow you will know. You can't hide it. They will resist or ignore your leadership because they expect you to bail out at the first sign of trouble or leave at the first opportunity for more pay.

Passion for the mission is not passion for self. It is not passion for profit (although in business, profit is a good and necessary thing), and it is not passion for being the biggest or most prominent (whether a business or a church). Passion for the mission endures through the ups and downs of the economy or when several hundred people leave because the church down the street has a cooler youth ministry. When Merck & Company decided to develop and give away Mectizan, a drug that cured river blindness in Africa (negatively affecting the bottom line by hundreds of millions of dollars because the people who needed it couldn't pay for it), it was because their mission was, and still is, higher than profits. According to George W. Merck, president of Merck from 1925 to 1950, "We try never to forget that medicine is for people. It is not for profits. The profits follow."[13]

When Blake Mycoskie was in Argentina playing a rich man's game—polo—he was moved by the thousands of poor kids there who didn't have shoes. However, he moved past emotion to passion and founded TOMS Shoes, a for-profit company whose mission as headlined on its website is: "With every pair you purchase, TOMS will give a pair of new shoes to a child in need. One for One.™"[14]

Ask most anyone under age thirty—they'll know all about TOMS shoes and probably have a pair. In August 2010, Mycoskie was back in Argentina, not to play polo, but to give away the one millionth pair of shoes! Wow! Now that's passion for the mission.

Through its long history, Merck has faced some tough years, and TOMS will undoubtedly run into hard times at some point. But guess what? They have made it and will make it through. Why? Authors Kouzes and Posner give us the answer in *The Leadership Challenge*: people get "through the tough times" because they have a "strong sense of . . . purpose."[15]

Passion for the mission—you have to have it if you are going to lead. Do you? Or are you just trying to make a buck?

#2—Passion for change. In addition to passion for the mission, Kouzes and Posner also emphasize that leaders "must be agents of change."[16] So, if nothing is changing, you aren't leading. Let me repeat that: if nothing is changing in your organization, then you are not leading. In fact, *nobody* is leading. Your organization is leaderless and stagnant.

It doesn't matter what type of organization you are part of—large corporation, small business, church or nonprofit, technology company, service provider, or goods producer—change is happening all around you, and there is not one thing you can do to stop it. You can take the bull by the horns and shape the change, or you can sit back and let the change shape you. It's your choice. But if you are a true leader, there is only one choice—LEAD THE CHANGE! And if you are going to lead change, you have to have passion for it.

Great leaders are energized by change. They expect it and embrace it. If you as the leader don't embrace it, don't expect the organization to.

Where would IBM be today if it were still relying on mainframe computers as their primary profit stream? AT&T is booming, but it's not because of landline telephones—it's a wireless world now. If you are in the music business and are hoping to survive selling those nearly obsolete round things called CDs, forget it. You are stuck in the eighties. Netflix took out Blockbuster, and the Internet is taking out newspapers by the hundreds. In the church world, Generation X is abandoning denominational loyalties, and Millennials are leaving rock band mega-churches for candles, incense, and quiet acoustics. Change is everywhere and relentless. You can't avoid it. That is not a light at the end of the tunnel; it's a runaway train that is going to run over you if you don't have passion for change.

This is going to sound harsh and may make you angry, but here's the truth: if you by nature don't like change, it is going to be hard for you to lead because leading is all about change. You can supervise, you can manage, and you can contribute in other ways, but you can't lead. So if you don't have passion for change, you better catch it quick or get a new job because the world around you is changing. The '50s aren't coming back! Neither are the '90s.

#3—Passion for people. You don't lead machines, you don't lead software, and you don't lead buildings. You lead people. Leading is always about people. So if you are going to lead, you better have passion for people. If you don't really care much about the people you are trying to lead, they'll know it and will only follow you kicking and screaming because they have to. You will have to drag them along, and you'll be worn out long before you get to the finish line.

Passion for people doesn't mean you are a soft leader who walks around saying, "Can't we all just get along?" It doesn't mean you are trying to please everyone all the time. That is a sure formula for failure. Vince Lombardi, one of the toughest leaders—by reputation—of all time said: "I don't necessarily have to like my players and associates, but as a leader I must love them. Love is loyalty, love is teamwork, love respects the dignity of the individual. This is the strength of any organization."[17]

Does that statement shatter your image of him? Lombardi won five NFL championships not just because he had passion for football and winning (which he did), but because he had passion for his players. Love for them was the strength of his organization.

In one of my leadership roles, three to four times a year I gave a state-of-the-company briefing to all employees at all levels (hourly, salaried, union, non-union, all three shifts). Because I truly loved the company and the people, at the end of one of the sessions, I finished something like this: "Thanks for listening. Let's all go have a productive day. I love all of you." Yes, I did! I'm sure I violated all kinds of rules about what CEOs should say to employees. It just came out. It wasn't in the script, but it was in my heart, so I said it. What was the feedback? Over and over I heard, "Dick, the main thing they remember is that you love them. Don't stop telling them."

Lombardi was right. Too bad I didn't learn this earlier in my career. (If I had loved those first people, maybe they wouldn't have hated me.)

Scientists and engineers (like yours truly) are generally thought not to be *people persons*. After all, they sit around talking about formulas and experiments and writing technical papers that only three other people on planet Earth can understand. However, Albert Einstein, the greatest scientist of the twentieth century, said that "man is here for the sake of other men."[18] This is the guy who won the 1921 Nobel Prize for Physics and is considered by many to be the father of modern physics. It sounds to me like he had passion for people.

In his book *Getting Naked* (it's okay to read it; it's about transparency, not nudity), Patrick Lencioni writes, "There is nothing more attractive and admirable than people who willingly and cheerfully set their egos aside and make the needs of others more important than their own."[19] That sounds an awful lot like what the apostle Paul wrote in his letter to the Philippians almost 2,000 years ago: "Do nothing out of selfish ambition or vain conceit, but in humility consider others better than yourselves. Each of you should look not only to your own interests, but also to the interests of others" (Philippians 2:3–4 NIV).

It is not Dick Wells saying you need to have passion for people, it's *God*. I've learned it's a good idea to pay attention to whatever He has to say.

Leaders lead people, and to lead effectively you need to have passion for them. Do you? If you don't, leading is always going to be a chore instead of a joy.

#4—Passion for personal excellence. No organization ever rises above the level of its leadership. The leader is the lid—always! If you want an excellent organization, you have to be an excellent leader. If your leadership is mediocre, your organization will be mediocre. If your leadership is erratic, your organization will be erratic. If your leadership is based primarily on your personality and charisma, you won't achieve anything that endures beyond your tenure. The performance and accomplishments of your organization will never—on a long-term basis—exceed the level of your leadership. Great, enduring organizations will always have great leadership. It's up to you. Your passion for leadership must include passion for personal excellence.

Everything in life that is hard (like leadership) must be pursued diligently if you want to be excellent at it. Golf is hard; excellent golfers work hard. Playing the piano is hard; an excellent pianist works hard. A garden fit for the cover of *Better Homes and Gardens* takes hard work. It is not easy to be excellent at anything. Excellence requires passion, and leadership is no exception. That is why Scripture says, "If God has given you leadership ability, take the responsibility seriously" (Romans 12:8 NLT).

If you are serious about your leadership responsibility, you will have passion to continuously become a better leader, always striving to raise the level of your leadership. Is it worth the effort? King Solomon said it is: "Do you see a man who excels in his work? He will stand before kings; He will not stand before unknown men" (Proverbs 22:29 NKJV).

Great leaders have a passion for personal excellence. They spend a lot of time pursuing it. Why? Because they understand that their organizations are never going to be more excellent than they are.

#5—Passion for honoring God. If you are a Christian, whether leading a business or a ministry, there is a lot more at stake than your reputation or your organization's performance. God's honor is at stake. It doesn't matter whether you are leading a team of four or five clerks in a small retail store or leading a corporation with 10,000 employees, people are watching you. Many are skeptical, wondering if you are the real deal or just another hypocritical churchgoer. That is why Paul said, "And whatever you do, whether in word or deed, do it all in the name of the Lord Jesus" (Colossians 3:17 NIV). I'm pretty sure that "whatever you do" includes how you lead.

Unfortunately, the more successful we are, the more prone we are to lead in our own name, for our own honor, instead of God's. Success brings with it the high risk of "look what I have accomplished." Pride, a sense of entitlement, and an attitude of invincibility and infallibility can easily beset a successful leader. Scripture is full of warnings about the dangers of pride and self-exaltation:

> Pride goes before destruction, a haughty spirit before a fall. (Proverbs 16:18 NIV)

> The eyes of the arrogant man will be humbled and the pride of men brought low; the Lord alone will be exalted. (Isaiah 2:11 NIV)

Nehemiah was a leader who knew well these warnings. He had a high position in the king's service and would later become governor of Jerusalem. Throughout his leadership journey, however, he never forgot that he was successful because:

> The gracious hand of my God was upon me. (Nehemiah 2:8 NIV)

> The hand of my God had been favorable to me. (Nehemiah 2:18 NIV)

> The God of heaven will give us success. (Nehemiah 2:20 NIV)

Success did not spoil Nehemiah. Don't let it spoil you.

FAUX PASSIONS

Faux is the French word for "false" or "fake." Faux pearls are not real; faux furs are not real. Faux marble looks like real marble, but it's not. They are imitations, and they can fool us if we aren't looking out for them. Imitations are fine in a lot of instances. Faux marble looks great in the foyer. However, there are faux passions that we sometimes believe are necessary for leadership, but they are not only *un*necessary, they sometimes make it harder or impossible to lead.

Faux Passion #1—Sentiment. I grew up in Oklahoma, so my boyhood dream was to be a cowboy or a baseball player. (Duh! Mickey Mantle was from Oklahoma.) Doesn't every kid think "When I grow up I'm going to be a _____"? In high school, my love was basketball. But does that mean I should have been a coach? I fixed my coaching itch by coaching the Red Raiders (fifth- and sixth-grade boys) for a few years. We were terrible and didn't win many games—blame the coach. Today, I still want to be a cowboy (PBR bull rider; about that, my wife uses the word "stupid"). I don't follow baseball too much but still love basketball, especially March Madness. (I finished sixth out of fourteen in my family's bracket this year.)

It would be easy for me to confuse my sentiment for these things with passion for them. Sentiment and passion are not the same things, although a lot of amateur psychologists (unhappy in their adult lives) try to make them the same. Even if you talk to a professional, in spite of what your therapist may say, childhood dreams and sentimental memories are not often the answer to adult fulfillment, and they have little to do with your ability or what you will be passionate about as an adult. If they are the same, great! But chances are they won't be.

Faux Passion #2—Loving the task. By education I am an aerospace engineer. I went to school at Georgia Tech because it was the only place I could afford (in-state tuition and the co-op work program). Though as a boy I didn't build model airplanes or dream of going to the moon, I chose aerospace engineering because it was the 1960s, and the US was in a space race with the Russians. I liked the idea of beating the Russians, and aerospace offered a lot of job security, so aerospace it was. It didn't take me long to discover that I didn't really love the task of engineering and, frankly, was only average at it (at best). However, I discovered that I did love the challenge of leading a team to design, build, test, and certify a new aircraft. I didn't love the task, but I did love the challenge of leading, so I worked happily in the aerospace industry for more than thirty-five years.

It is great if you love the product or program of your organization, but you don't have to love it to lead it. Louis Gerstner Jr. left RJR Nabisco (cigarettes and Oreos) in 1993 to become CEO of IBM (mainframe computers). Do you think he loved computers more than Oreos? I suspect he didn't love either one, but he did have passion for "trying to build organizations that allow for hierarchy but at the same time bring people together for problem solving, regardless of where they are positioned in the organization."[20] Gerstner had passion for leading, and *that's* the passion a leader must have!

Do you suppose Nehemiah loved hauling rocks to build a wall more than he liked living in the king's palace? Was he an excellent stonemason? No. He wasn't even a mediocre stonemason. As cupbearer to the king, he loved and knew the difference between a good Riesling or Merlot, but granite or limestone? He didn't know—and I imagine he didn't much care. He was likely one of the worst wall builders on the team. Undoubtedly, he was ecstatic the morning he got out of bed with no more rocks to move. What he had was a great passion for the mission and for the people in Jerusalem. That gave him motivation to lead, and he led well. As John Maxwell notes, "A leader with great passion and few skills always outperforms a leader with great skills and no passion."[21]

I didn't have to love airplanes to have a passion for leading an aerospace company. Gerstner didn't need to have passion for computers to lead IBM. Nehemiah didn't have to be excited about building walls to have passion for the walls to be rebuilt. If you love the task—great! If you are called to lead, passion for leading and for a greater purpose is what you need, no matter what the task.

Faux Passion #3—Emotion. When Nehemiah heard that the walls in Jerusalem were down, he "sat down and wept." It stirred him intensely. More importantly, the fire of passion was lit within him. How do we know it was passion?

- Because the fire didn't go out after a few days—it got hotter
- Because Nehemiah couldn't ignore it—he had to do something
- Because he was willing to take a great risk to see it accomplished

Emotions have a way of going cold after a few days. Or if they continue to rage, it is usually about self. Emotions tend to be explosive, expressive, and exhausting—unlike passion. Passion will quietly energize you to action, and that is why it is essential for leadership. Great leadership is driven by passion, not emotion. In fact, emotional leadership is often more destructive than effective. As a leader, don't get the two mixed up.

PASSION: WHERE DO YOU FIND IT?

There is no pat answer to this question. I Googled "finding your passion" and found a three-step plan, a five-step plan, a seven-question plan, and a five-minute plan. All were helpful, but none were certain. Why? Because passion is not something you find. Rather, it finds you, or catches you, or calls out to you—take your pick.

In Nehemiah's case, his passion to rebuild the walls of Jerusalem was *"put into my heart"* by God (Nehemiah 2:12 NIV). The heart is where passion resides, catches fire, burns hot, and leads to action. There is a phrase we often use to encourage people to greater effort: "Put your heart into it!" I've heard it a thousand times from coaches, teachers, bosses, and preachers. However, where there is passion, that particular admonition is not necessary because the heart is already into it.

Although there is no formula for finding passion, there are some things that will help you recognize your passion:

- More than it *can* be done, or would be *good* to do, passion is something you intensely feel *should* be done and *must* be done. Your passion will really matter to you. (Read *Visioneering* by Andy Stanley or *Wild Goose Chase* by Mark Batterson.)
- True passion, when in action, will fill your tank, not drain it. You may become physically exhausted, but emotionally and spiritually you will be energized.
- You have a sense that if you don't act on your passion, you will have deep regrets later in life. (As I write Nehemiah's story, I have no idea if it will ever be published or if even one copy will be sold. I am writing because I know for sure that God has put this in my heart, and I will have deep regrets if I don't do it.)
- The embers of emotion go cold quickly, but the embers of passion stay warm for a long time. One squeeze of the bellows is all it takes to stoke up the fire. How long has this "thing you

must do" had a grip on you? (This book has been in my heart
for more than fifteen years.)

∷ Pay attention to what the people who know you best and love
you the most are saying to you. God may be using them to
help you recognize your passion.

My passion to tell Nehemiah's story was birthed in my passion for
leadership. How do I know I have passion for leadership? First, a leadership vacuum drives me crazy. I do not have to be in charge, but put me in
a setting where no one is in charge, and I can't stand it. I'll step in. Second,
abusive, self-centered, ineffective leadership drives me up the wall. "It doesn't
have to be this way," my heart is screaming. Third, I believe that in organizations, leadership trumps everything. As I said earlier, no organization ever
rises above the level of its leadership. If leadership is that important (and it
is!), then leaders better have passion for it. Finally, I love to help a team of
people *pull it off*. It doesn't much matter to me what the *it* is. If they have
a mission, a vision, and a plan, I want to help them get to the finish line.

So what's your passion? If you don't know, I hope you'll discover it soon.
If you are in leadership—and if you're reading this book, you probably are
in some way—I hope Nehemiah's story will give you passion to raise the
level of your leadership.

Leadership STONE ② KEEP YOUR TANK FULL . . . OF PASSION.

Nehemiah's reaction to Hanani's report that the "wall of Jerusalem
is broken down, and its gates have been burned with fire" triggered much
more than a sentimental tugging at his heart or an emotional breakdown.
It set off a passion to do something, which wouldn't let go of him. It was
personal. It set his *soul on fire* to take action that was both risky and incon-
venient. That's the true kind of passion leaders need. Without it, leading is
drudgery, strength-sapping, and emotionally draining.

Are you trying to lead, but it seems like a never-ending trek up a
steep hill?

Ask yourself: Do I really have passion for leading?

Do you have *fire in your soul* for the mission?

For change?

For people?

For personal excellence?

For honoring God?

Has your passion cooled because of circumstances or the difficulty of the task?

Is there something you *must do* but haven't started?

Will you have regrets if you don't?

What is stopping you?

Whatever you lead needs you to have true passion. Your company needs it. Your church needs it. Your family needs it. If leading has become "just a job," ask God to take a match and light the fire of leadership passion in your soul. Do it today! ■

3

"WAIT" IS A FOUR-LETTER WORD

All things will be clear and distinct to the man who does not hurry;
haste is blind and improvident.[22]

TITUS LIVIUS

What in the world is taking Nehemiah so long? We arrived in Susa almost four months ago, and we're still here, eating, drinking, and sleeping too much. (I guess that's not all bad, but I have gained ten pounds.) I don't see very much of Nehemiah. Sometimes I almost feel like he's avoiding me. He has the excuse of being busy with his cupbearer duties, but even when he's not serving the king, he hangs out in his chamber all by himself. "Praying," he says. When we do see him, he grills us for hours with questions:

How long is the wall?

How high should it be?

Do the people there want it rebuilt, or are they content to continue living as is?

He obviously has some thoughts about rebuilding it, but he's sure keeping most of them to himself. Besides, I don't really see how he could do it. After all, he is a slave. He can't just pick up and go anywhere he wants to or do much of anything without the king's permission. There's no way the king would let him leave. He's too valuable and trusted in the court by both the king and the queen.

All of this is complicated by the fact that there's no reason the king should want the walls rebuilt, and even if he did, he would hardly consider Nehemiah the man for the job. My brother's a cupbearer, for crying out loud. He doesn't know anything about wall design and construction. The only thing Nehemiah has going for him is that the king trusts him—probably the only Jew Artaxerxes does trust!

Still, I can't help but wonder what Nehemiah has in mind since he seems so preoccupied with Jerusalem. When I ask Nehemiah if he has a plan, all he says is, "Wait, the time isn't right." All his praying won't do much good. God had most of the Jews hauled off to slavery more than 140 years ago, and I don't see that He has changed His mind about us. Maybe Nehemiah's connections to the king won't help Jerusalem after all. Not if Nehemiah is unwilling to make a move.

Eventually we may just have to forget the whole thing and head home. Sounds awful! I hate that trip, but I can't stay here forever.

NEHEMIAH'S JOURNAL

"In the month of Kislev in the twentieth year, while I was in the citadel of Susa, Hanani, one of my brothers, came from Judah with some other men . . . . In the month of Nisan in the twentieth year of King Artaxerxes, when wine was brought for him, I took the wine and gave it to the king." (Nehemiah 1:1–2; 2:1 NIV)

[Note: The Jewish month of Kislev corresponds to our November–December, and the Jewish month of Nisan corresponds to March–April. That means roughly four months passed between Nehemiah 1:1 and Nehemiah 2:1.]

⁑ ⁑ ⁑ ⁑

FALSE STARTS

I ran track in high school—the 440-yard sprint, a quarter mile of lung-busting, muscle-burning torture. I wasn't fast enough to impress anyone. I never won a race and barely scored enough points to letter. But I enjoyed the camaraderie on the team and the sound of the starter's gun. It also helped that track season was springtime, and there were always a few cute girls at track meets.

Each race started with: "On your mark . . . get set . . . " BANG! "On your mark" was the command to get in the starting blocks in a relaxed position. "Get set" meant to get ready to explode out of the starting blocks by raising your rear end and leaning forward with your body coiled like a spring. The normal pause between "get set" and BANG was about two seconds, but it always seemed much longer. With muscles tight and ready to go and emotions taut and on the edge, it was easy to jump the gun—to go before the BANG. Jumping the gun was called a *false start*. False starts were a bummer for everyone, especially for the guilty runner. Everyone had to go through the whole "on your mark" thing all over again, but the guilty runner was now in double jeopardy because a second false start meant disqualification. In 2010, the rules were tightened to *one false start and you're out*. That's the way it often is in leadership: jump the gun even once, and you're out.

Considering the magnitude of his request to go to Jerusalem and rebuild the walls, Nehemiah knew he would likely get only one chance with the king. If he jumped the gun and asked too soon—before his planning was done and he could answer all the king's questions—he would more than likely hear "no."

Whatever the cause, it's hard to wait for the gun when you are fired up and ready to go. And it's especially hard for leaders who by nature are trigger happy for action. It was hard for Nehemiah; it is hard for you and me. Yet as hard as it is, waiting is often the right thing to do, especially when God is the One calling us to do something. We seem always to be in a hurry. God almost never is.

MAKE HASTE SLOWLY

Hanani showed up in Susa in late November to visit Nehemiah. After hugs and some small talk—"How are you; how was the trip?"—Nehemiah asked about the thing that mattered most to him: "What's the situation back in Jerusalem?"

"Horrible," responded Hanani, "things are in really bad shape. The walls are still down, and the people are living in fear, shame, and disgrace."

Nehemiah responded like any faithful Jew, right? "Get the camels ready. Pack up. We'll leave for Jerusalem at first light tomorrow morning."

Actually, that is the way most red-blooded twenty-first century leaders would respond, but *not* Nehemiah. Instead of leaping into action, he "sat down and wept . . . mourned for a number of days, fasting and praying" (Nehemiah 1:4 HCSB). In fact, "a number of days" dragged on into December, January, February, and March. Four long months went by with no action. He didn't appear to be a decisive, take-charge leader. In today's world, the business channel talking heads already would be questioning whether he was the "right choice" to lead the turn-around of Jerusalem Inc.

We are all about action. New presidents are measured by what they accomplish in the first one hundred days. We expect new coaches to win the first year, new CEOs to be profitable the first quarter, and new pastors to fill the auditorium on the first Sunday (or at least the second). Four months of no action brings out the armchair quarterbacks, fires up the second-guessers and turns on the skeptics. There aren't many places where "praying" is an acceptable answer to "What have you been doing for four months?" Not when the walls are down. Not when the people are in shame and disgrace. Not when they have been waiting for 142 years for someone to rebuild the walls.

Waiting stinks. How many people—especially men—do you know who are good at waiting? Don't ask my wife about me. Waiting is hard. It's not natural, especially waiting patiently (as opposed to the pacing-the-floor-while-grumbling kind of waiting). Most of us are not good at waiting, and we don't like it, but the wisdom of centuries endorses and applauds it:

- 3,000 years ago—King David said, "Indeed, none of those who wait for You will be ashamed." (Psalm 25:3 NASB95)
- 2,400 years ago—Prophet Habakkuk: "This vision is for a future time. It describes the end, and it will be fulfilled. If it seems

slow in coming, wait patiently, for it will surely take place. It will not be delayed." (Habakkuk 2:3 NLT)

- 1,950 years ago—Luke the Physician: "But don't begin until you count the cost. For who would begin construction of a building without first calculating the cost to see if there is enough money to finish it?" (Luke 14:28 NLT)
- 250 years ago—Benjamin Franklin: "Make haste slowly."
- 100 years ago—Arthur Henderson: "Therefore, let us not despair, but instead, survey the position, consider carefully the action we must take, and then address ourselves to our common task in a mood of sober resolution and quiet confidence, without haste and without pause."[23]
- Twenty-first century—Malcolm Gladwell: "What do we tell our children? Haste makes waste. Look before you leap. Stop and think. Don't judge a book by its cover. We believe that we are always better off gathering as much information as possible and spending as much time as possible in deliberation."[24]

"Make haste slowly." Was he joking? Benjamin Franklin would never have survived if he had had to face the firestorm of criticism on cable news or the blogosphere. On the other hand, he also wouldn't have survived if "haste made waste" and produced a tragic mistake.

For four months Hanani waited for Nehemiah to do something. Hanani probably didn't like waiting any more than you and I do. He was in a hurry to get back to Jerusalem and get the job done. Yet Nehemiah apparently was in no hurry at all. Or so it seemed. As we'll see, Nehemiah was very busy during the four months. Before the wall in Jerusalem could be raised one stone at a time, there were stones in Susa that had to be moved out of the way, and they were too big for Nehemiah to move.

ONLY GOD CAN MOVE SOME STONES

According to leadership expert Fred Smith, "the key to positive action is knowing the difference between a problem and a fact of life. A problem is something that can be solved. A fact of life is something that must be accepted."[25] In other words, the "facts of life" cannot be changed, so don't bother trying. That is great advice in most situations. For example, except with the Amish, cars have replaced horse-drawn buggies as the primary mode of family transportation. Because there are only about 250,000 Amish in the US, the market for buggy whips is relatively small. That is a "fact of life" you cannot change. Therefore, a business growth strategy based on dominating the buggy whip market is certain to fail. Now it is possible that at some point in the future we could run out of oil, and horse-drawn buggies could make a comeback. For now, however, cars are it, and that's a fact of life you better accept.

Facts of life are stones that man cannot move. In the introduction, I set the odds at 1,000 to 1 against Nehemiah successfully rebuilding the walls of Jerusalem. The truth is, he faced so many facts of life that the odds against him were likely even greater. It was a long shot that he could get to Jerusalem to try to rebuild the walls. Why? As Hanani's Journal observed, Nehemiah was a slave. The only way Nehemiah could go to Jerusalem for any reason was to get the king's permission. But his presence in the court was crucial to the king's daily life. Not a single glass of wine or platter of food was set before the king unless Nehemiah had overseen its preparation and tested it personally. Was there anyone that the king would trust enough to fill in for Nehemiah? Even if he could find someone, why should he bother? The king was a pagan. Jerusalem was not his heart home—not spiritually, not politically, not in any way at all. He had no motive to let Nehemiah so much as visit Jerusalem, let alone stay long enough to rebuild the walls. Nehemiah was going to need a lot of help moving this stone out of the way.

There were some other facts of life that made this whole idea a "no-go" from the beginning. Nehemiah had no experience building walls. He was a palace servant, not a civil engineer. Pouring wine takes a deft touch; building walls takes muscles and calloused hands, and oh yes, resources—you can't build a wall with empty wine skins. No experience . . . no calluses . . . no resources . . . adds up to "no way." Not to mention that Jerusalem was 900 hundred miles away, and it is doubtful Nehemiah had ever even visited the broken-down city. He was clueless. He was as unlikely a candidate as Chef Emeril Lagasse of Food Channel would be today. But as Paul Harvey would say, "the rest of the story" was an even bigger fact of life, a bigger stone that had to be moved.

The "rest of the story" is recorded in Ezra, chapter 4. At an earlier time in King Artaxerxes's reign—before Nehemiah arrived on the scene—the Jews had, without permission, begun the task of rebuilding the walls. Their enemies (some of the same ones Nehemiah would encounter) attempted to stop the work by appealing to the king:

> (This is a copy of the letter they sent him.) To King Artaxerxes, From your servants, the men of Trans-Euphrates: The king should know that the Jews who came up to us from you have gone to Jerusalem and are rebuilding that rebellious and wicked city. They are restoring the walls and repairing the foundations. Furthermore, the king should know that if this city is built and its walls are restored, no more taxes, tribute or duty will be paid, and the royal revenues will suffer. Now since we are under obligation to the palace and it is not proper for us to see the king dishonored, we are sending this message to inform the king, so that a search may be made in the archives of your pre-decessors. In these records you will find that this city is a rebellious city, troublesome to kings and provinces, a place of rebellion from ancient times. That is why this city was destroyed. We inform the king that if this city is built and its walls are restored, you will be left with nothing in Trans-Euphrates. (Ezra 4:11-16 NIV)

Their strategy worked:

> The king sent this reply: . . . The letter you sent us has been read and translated in my presence. I issued an order and a search was made, and it was found that this city has a long history of revolt against kings and has been a place of rebellion and sedition. Jerusalem has had powerful kings ruling over the whole of Trans-Euphrates, and taxes, tribute and duty were paid to them. Now issue an order to these men to stop work, so that this city will not be rebuilt until I so order. (Ezra 4:17-21 NIV)

The king ordered the work stopped, and it was. The walls remained a pile of rubble. In order to rebuild the walls of Jerusalem, King Artaxerxes would have to reverse the previous order prohibiting the work. Even though the king left the door open ("this city will not be rebuilt until I so order") for rebuilding the walls, was it likely? Kings didn't often change their minds; it was considered a sign of weakness. So the king's previous decision was another big stone that Nehemiah couldn't move. Nehemiah had a lot of facts of life staring him in the face. He was a slave to a pagan king, had an important job, and could not easily be replaced. He had no experience and no resources. And on top of all that, the king would have to change his mind and revoke an earlier "stop work" order.

It is no wonder Nehemiah didn't jump on the first camel to Jerusalem. He had a lot to think and pray about—easily four months' worth. He wasn't ready to just accept the facts of life and get on with his cupbearing. He knew the odds were against him, but he also knew that the odds don't mean a thing to God:

> A king's heart is a water channel in the LORD's hand: He directs it wherever He chooses. (Proverbs 21:1 HCSB)

> Ah, Lord God! You Yourself made the heavens and earth by Your great power and with Your outstretched arm. Nothing is too difficult for You! (Jeremiah 32:17 HCSB)

Most important of all, he knew what God was calling him to do: "I had not told anyone what my God had put in my heart to do" (Nehemiah 2:11–12 NIV). Considering God's role, the odds were actually in Nehemiah's favor, no matter what the facts of life were.

When your leadership passion gets fired up to do something, one of the reasons to look before you leap is there may be some stones—some facts of life—only God can move. What should you do? First, be sure of your calling. Then follow Nehemiah's example: pray. For how long? I can't answer that for you, but Nehemiah prayed for four months. Start with that, and see where God takes you. For instance:

> I waited patiently for the LORD; And He inclined to me and heard my cry. (Psalm 40:1 NASB95)

> Since ancient times no one has heard, no ear has perceived, no eye has seen any God besides you, who acts on behalf of those who wait for him. (Isaiah 64:4 NIV)

If you think waiting is hard, try butting your head against a fact of life. You'll wear out and give up before you accomplish anything. Then you'll begin to question whether God really called you to the task. Discouraged and defeated, you'll slip back into your ordinary comfortable life, and some wall that needs to be rebuilt will remain a pile of rubble. Isn't waiting—a little patience and a lot of prayer—a better alternative? God doesn't expect you to move the stones only He can move. He doesn't even expect you to try. And for sure, He doesn't want you to listen to the critics who trash you for lack of action. Instead of wasting your time trying to move stones you can't move, put your effort into prayer and moving the stones you can. Leave the rest to God.

MOVE THE STONES YOU CAN

In his excellent book *Visioneering*, Andy Stanley says of God's part in getting things done, "Our responsibility is to do what we know to do, and wait for Him to fill in the blanks."[26] Nehemiah was a great example of "do what we know to do." First, he knew he should pray, and he did, fervently. Second, he knew he should put his passion to work moving the stones he could. Before there were any leadership books or leadership summits to learn from, Nehemiah knew that he shouldn't sit back and wait for God to do everything. In addition to his fervent prayer, it is safe to say that Nehemiah did at least these three things during his four months of waiting:

- He sought counsel.
- He did as much advance thinking and planning as he could.
- He anticipated questions.

Seek counsel. Nehemiah knew from Scripture that "plans fail when there is no counsel, but with many advisers they succeed" (Proverbs 15:22 HCSB). Though he had not seen the piles of rubble himself, he had access to his brother Hanani and the others who had just arrived from Jerusalem. No doubt, he had a long list of questions for them:

- How long is the wall, and how high should it be rebuilt?
- Can the piles of rubble be used, or will new stones have to be brought in?
- Since the gates are burned, how close are the nearest stands of timber?
- What resources are available—donkeys, carts, pulleys?
- Do the people really want to rebuild the walls, or are they content with conditions as they are?
- Who will oppose the project, and how fiercely will they try to stop it?

In addition to the four months of waiting in Susa, Nehemiah later had about four months of travel from Susa to Jerusalem to continue asking questions and seeking counsel. I suspect Hanani and the others were tired of questions and really glad when they got to Jerusalem so Nehemiah could see for himself.

According to the late Stephen Covey, "communication is the most important skill in life."[27] In our star-struck culture, we are quick to hang the "great communicator" tag on the charismatic mega-church pastors or leaders whose preaching and oratory keep people on the edge of their seats. But actually, the two most important communication skills for leaders are:

- being a great listener, and
- using questions to gain information and reach conclusions and/or consensus.

These two skills are far more important than eloquent speaking. The people you are trying to lead will long remember the day you asked them for information or "what would you do?" advice. They will not forget the times you sat and genuinely listened to their input. Your spellbinding speech or sermon of last week will be forgotten soon after your spellbinding speech or sermon of this week, which will be forgotten soon after . . . you get the idea. The ability to speak eloquently may gather a crowd, but it won't garner followers.

About "wise counsel," George Burns, the popular cigar-smoking comedian of the World War II and Baby Boomer generations, had this to say: "Too bad that all the people who really know how to run the country are busy driving taxi cabs and cutting hair."[28] A New York cabbie may be a great source of counsel for how to find the Empire State Building but not so great for how to rebuild a wall in Jerusalem . . . or a business . . . or a church. It's easy to get advice, not so easy to get *good* advice. An overall principle for seeking counsel is the old adage, "Consider the source." Here are things I consider:

- Are they speaking from firsthand successful experience, not just theoretical or academic knowledge? I want to talk to people who have been on the front lines of leadership and been successful there.
- Do they have a personal agenda? Be careful if they have something significant to gain or lose.

- Have they experienced some failure? The road to humility always has a failure marker or two. The best counsel will come from people who are trying to help you, not impress you.
- Do I know them personally? If I don't, I seek input about them from people I do know and trust.
- Are their values consistent with mine? Nehemiah had this to say about his brother: "He was a faithful man who feared God" (Nehemiah 7:2 HCSB). A faithful man who fears God has values consistent with mine and will get my undivided attention if he meets the first four criteria.

If I can't find a source of counsel that meets all five of these criteria, I am cautious. Getting a second opinion is always a good idea. Remember that Proverbs 15:22 says plans succeed with *many* advisors.

Advance planning. In their best-selling book of 2002, *Execution* (one of my personal favorites and a must-read for leaders), Larry Bossidy and Ram Charan make the following oh-so-true statement: "Unless you translate big thoughts into concrete steps for action, they're pointless."[29] For four months, Nehemiah had prayed, asking God to move the stones only God could move. He had sought counsel, picking Hanani's brain about the conditions in Jerusalem, asking him a thousand questions about the wall, the people, the opposition, and probably even the weather. At some point, Nehemiah became certain of his calling—"what . . . God had put in my heart to do" (Nehemiah 2:12 NIV). Now he had a choice to make: sit back with an it's-out-of-my-hands-I've-done-all-I-can-do attitude, or ask, "What more can I do; what concrete steps for action can I take?"

Great leaders are always looking for another stone they can move. "Leave no stone unturned"[30] is an ancient and fundamental operating principle for effective leaders. From my own experiences and observations, there is always another stone a leader can move or turn. It may not be the biggest or most important stone (the one or two only God can move), but there is rarely a time when all you can do is throw up your hands and sit in despair. Winston Churchill was right when he said, "Let our advance worrying become advance thinking and planning."[31] So for Nehemiah, it was time to begin as much planning—"concrete steps for action"—as he could with the information he had.

I suspect Nehemiah was not a rookie planner. The elaborate meals served to King Artaxerxes weren't thrown together at the last minute. He knew "failing to plan is planning to fail." The last person in Persia anyone wanted to disappoint was the king. Give him a bad piece of meat, and the gallows or chopping block was only one bite away. There was a lot of detail planning he couldn't do until he arrived in Jerusalem to see things firsthand. However, he could:

- Choose a route for the journey (straight west across the desert or northwest along the rivers),
- Make a list of provisions for the trip,
- Decide who he would recommend to be in charge while he was gone,
- Think about what he would do first when he arrived in Jerusalem,
- Make a list of things he needed from the king, and
- Formulate answers to questions the king might ask [more on this later].

Execution effectively trashed the 1990s idea that leaders should spend their time having "big thoughts" and casting vision while leaving the planning and execution to others. The book opens with this resounding statement: "Many people regard execution as detail work that's beneath the dignity of a business leader. That's wrong. To the contrary, it's the leader's most important job."[32] The *most important* job—wow! The authors go on to say that leaders who ignore planning and execution are "building houses without foundations."[33] Nehemiah did not have the advantage of *Execution* on his bookshelf, but he had something better—the wisdom of King Solomon: "The plans of the diligent lead surely to advantage" (Proverbs 21:5 NASB95).

So, a few thoughts about planning:

- While a vision without a plan is pointless, it is also true that planning without a vision is equally pointless. Philosopher and Hall of Fame baseball catcher Yogi Berra put it this way: "If you don't know where you're going, you'll end up somewhere else."[34]
- Strategic planning is the job of leadership; tactical planning is everybody's job—including the leaders. Leaders ignore planning or execution at their own peril.

- If it's not on paper, it's only an idea, not a plan. If it requires more than one person, takes more than one day, and has more than one task—write it down! (I know it's a paperless world now, so yes, your computer will do just fine.)
- If planning is not your strength, surround yourself with people who are great at it, but don't walk away from it. If you are the leader, it is your responsibility to make sure it is done and done well.
- The most effective plan will always be the team's plan. People will execute their own plan much more effectively than your plan even if your plan is better. It is the leader's job to make sure the team's plan has no fatal weak points.
- Planning is the easy part. Execution is much harder. Have you noticed how things always look easy on paper?

And one last thought about planning from General Dwight Eisenhower, one of the twentieth century's greatest leaders: "In preparing for battle I have always found that plans are useless, but planning is indispensable."[35]

Plans are made to change. That is why flexibility is such an important part of leadership. History is full of examples in which "sticking to the plan" instead of "changing the plan" extracted a high price. In December 1862, the Union army lost a key battle at Fredericksburg in large part because General Burnside wouldn't change his plan (read *Gods and Generals* by Jeff Shaara). Plans are put on paper (or computer)—instead of carved in stone—so they can be changed. By the way, I do mean *change* the plan, not discard it and operate without one.

Anticipate questions. At some point Nehemiah was going to have to ask King Artaxerxes for permission to go to Jerusalem. All of us have faced a similar situation. We wanted to launch a new product line or ministry. We wanted to modernize a 1950s factory or refurbish the preschool facilities. We wanted to open a satellite church. However, between us and our goal stood a CEO, a board of directors or elders, a congregation, or a bank. To get it done, we needed permission or money or more staff or time off. Like Nehemiah, we prayed and planned and sought counsel while waiting patiently for the opportunity to make our case. Finally, the big day arrived. With a fresh haircut and a new suit, and PowerPoint charts that were concise, clear, and compelling, we confidently made our pitch, fully expecting a standing ovation and enthusiastic support. Wanting to appear humble, we concluded with, "Are there any questions?" Sure enough—much to our amazement—there were. Because we had not anticipated the question or questions, our sure thing started to unravel, and the big day ended with a disappointing "no" or "go back and do your homework."

"I don't know" or "I didn't think about that" are lousy answers to a king's question. For Nehemiah, the question from the king was a simple one: "How long will your journey take, and when will you get back?" (Nehemiah 2:6 NIV). "I'm not sure" would have been the end of the discussion, but Nehemiah had anticipated the question and was ready with an answer, so "it pleased the king to send me" (Nehemiah 2:6 NIV). Anticipating questions is a critically important part of the planning process, and it can be the difference between a joyful outcome or an unhappy one: "A man has joy in an apt answer" (Proverbs 15:23 NASB95).

Why is this so important? First, there will always be something you didn't think about. You may cover 99 percent of the subject and miss the 1 percent that can sink your proposal. Second, other people have a different perspective than you do. What is obvious to you is a mystery to them, or vice-versa. Third, someone in your audience may have information that you don't have. Nothing will halt a proposal faster than an "I didn't know that" response to a relevant and important comment or question.

There is no iron-clad formula for anticipating questions other than hard work, remembering that Proverbs 21:5 says it is the plans of the *diligent* that lead to advantage. Here are my suggestions for being diligent in your planning:

- Pre-brief your presentation/ideas with colleagues from three camps—(1) one that is very knowledgeable and involved; (2) one that is knowledgeable but neutral or skeptical, having no stake in the outcome; and (3) one that knows little and will ask those "dumb questions" that frustrate you, but expose weak points. Get their response to: What is missing? What isn't clear? Are we sure we have all the facts? What is our weakest point, and how can we strengthen it? Will we encounter active opposition for personal reasons, and how do we counter it?

- Follow Nehemiah's example. Don't ask your coworkers to wish you good luck. Rather, enter the king's chamber or CEO's office breathing a prayer to "Give your servant success today by granting him favor in the presence of this man" (Nehemiah 1:11). (We'll talk more about *favor* in chapter 4.)

Leadership STONE 3 DON'T JUMP THE GUN; DON'T WASTE THE WAIT.[36]

Waiting in the starting blocks is hard for most of us. Nehemiah was no exception. The walls of Jerusalem had been down for more than 140 years when Nehemiah became fired with passion to rebuild them. Nehemiah had to wait four months for the BANG. However, he wasn't just waiting; he was acting.

- Prayer is action.
- Planning is action.
- Seeking counsel is action.
- Anticipating questions is action.

He didn't jump the gun. As a result, "it pleased the king" to send him. How about you?

Are you actively waiting, or just procrastinating?

Are you praying about the stones only God can move?

Are you moving the stones you can?

While you wait, are you planning, seeking counsel, anticipating questions?

Are you gaining the experience and skills you will need to lead?

If "yes" comes today, are you ready to hit the trail for Jerusalem?

Are you in Hanani's position—waiting for your leader to take action?

What are you doing to support and encourage the leader while you wait?

Remember, a false start usually means losing the race or being disqualified altogether. But don't sit there doing nothing while you're waiting for the gun to go off. Plan . . . pray . . . ask questions . . . seek advice.

4

THE MOST IMPORTANT JOB
YOU'LL EVER HAVE

The king's favor is toward a servant who acts wisely,
but his anger is toward him who acts shamefully.
PROVERBS 14:35 NASB95

Nehemiah is quite the man around here. All I hear is how great he is and how the king respects and trusts him. He seems to be most everyone's favorite. Even though he has a high position, it's not just his position that seems to impress people. It's how he goes about his work that has won everyone over.

One thing I hear again and again is that he really knows his job and excels at what he does. His standard of performance is high for himself and for his staff. He expects a lot and leads by example. He hardly ever messes up, but when he does, he takes the blame himself. That's rare. Most of the other court officials spend their time trying to take credit for everything the king likes or shift the blame for what he doesn't like.

Nehemiah's kitchen staff love working for him. They know what he expects, and he makes sure they have what they need to get the job done. He treats them with respect, listens to their suggestions, praises their accomplishments, and pitches in to help when they get behind. Several of them have told me, "Nehemiah is our best boss ever."

I've noticed, too, that even though there are some other cupbearers, for the really big events—banquets, holidays, the queen's birthday—the king always wants Nehemiah in charge of preparations and serving of the meal. He is obviously the king's favorite. Hopefully, that will make a difference when Nehemiah raises the big question about the walls of Jerusalem. If Nehemiah doesn't come through, we might as well forget the whole thing and head back to Jerusalem because no one else will even try.

NEHEMIAH'S JOURNAL

"'O Lord, let your ear be attentive to the prayer of this your servant and to the prayer of your servants who delight in revering your name. Give your servant success today by granting him favor in the presence of this man.' I was cupbearer to the king." (Nehemiah 1:11 NIV)

:: :: :: ::

"HE'S ONE OF MY FAVORITES"

The Polo Club in Palm Desert (think palm trees, blue cloudless sky, low humidity, Ritz-Carlton, cool evening breezes) was the site of the opening reception for our corporation's annual meeting. All of the directors, corporate officers, key staff, and division presidents, along with their spouses, were there for three days of business in the mornings, fun in the afternoons, and dinner every evening.

It was my first time at the annual meeting so I was excited as my wife Dottie and I worked our way up the receiving line. After the Chief Human Resources Officer, Chief Legal Counsel, and Chief Financial Officer, we came to the second highest chief, the Chief Operating Officer. As we approached the COO, he offered a huge smile and made my day when he introduced me to his wife by saying, "This is Dick Wells. He runs our Nashville division, and he's one of my favorites." For about ten seconds my ego soared completely out of control until the COO's wife brought me down to earth by responding, "You say that about everyone." Anyway, it was nice while it lasted.

Let's be honest: don't we all want to be someone's favorite? We learn early in life the advantages of being a favorite. We strive to be the teacher's favorite or the coach's, and then at some point it's a girl or guy we hope to marry, and later the boss. If that striving is focused on serving, not manipulating, flattering, etc., it is a good thing. The Bible has many examples of men and women who had favor with men: "Joseph found favor in his master's sight and became his personal attendant" (Genesis 39:4 HCSB). Ruth, Esther, Samuel, and Daniel are others who had favor with men: Ruth with Boaz, Esther with King Xerxes, Samuel with the all the men of Israel, and Daniel with King Nebuchadnezzar's chief of staff.

The Bible also reveals there is such a thing as favor with God:

> By contrast, the boy Samuel grew in stature and in favor with the LORD and with men. (1 Samuel 2:26 HCSB)

> Then you will find favor and high regard in the sight of God and man. (Proverbs 3:1–4 HCSB)

> And Jesus grew in wisdom and stature, and in favor with God and men. (Luke 2:52 NIV)

There exists today a widely held belief that because we live and work in a world which often ignores or is sometimes even hostile to God, we cannot have favor with both God and man. By this thinking, if we have the favor of man, then we must be living and working in a way that doesn't please God, and we will not have His favor. Or if we live and work in a way that pleases God, there is no way for us to please man and have his favor. It's not true. Don't buy in to this false teaching. Scripture is clear that we can have favor with *both* God and man, and we should strive to do so. If Daniel could do it in Babylon, if Joseph could do it in Egypt, then we can do it in today's world.

Since this is a book focused on Nehemiah's leadership and is not intended to incite disputes about theology and doctrine, I will leave the subject of "favor with God" to the pastors and seminary professors who have given their lives to the study and understanding of Scripture. Whereas they can read Hebrew and Greek upside down and backwards, I have to rely on *Hebrew and Greek for Dummies*. Though I have personal convictions about when the favor of God is general, special, limited, earned, granted, and so on, I am narrowing my discussion here to Nehemiah's request for favor with the king.

"GRANT ME FAVOR"

I have personal experience seeking the favor of supervisors, vice-presidents, company presidents, CEOs, board chairmen, and business owners. And I have a lot of experience with others seeking my favor as I served in some of those same roles. I have been in Nehemiah's shoes. I know what it's like to breathe a prayer when entering a conference room full of corporate kings or Wall Street bankers. I have also been in the king's shoes. I know what predisposes a king to look with favor on the requestor even before the request is known.

Nehemiah ends chapter 1 of his story by breathing a prayer, asking God to grant him favor with the king. He was getting ready to ask for a leave of absence to rebuild Jerusalem. Nehemiah knew the king had few reasons, if any, to say "yes" and a lot of reasons to say "no." He really needed the king's favor because "when a king's face lights up, there is life; his favor is like a cloud with spring rain" (Proverbs 16:15 HCSB).

The context of Nehemiah 1:11 is important. Nehemiah's request for success and favor was not a spur of the moment impulse nor a prayer offered in panic. He sensed in his spirit that "today is the day." So he started his day by asking God to give him success, to grant him favor with the king. It was a very specific prayer. Success meant two things: (1) he needed the king to be predisposed with favor toward him so he would get a chance to make his request, and (2) he needed special favor, a "yes" from the king to his request. However, the most important thing was not what he asked for (success, favor, compassion, mercy), but how he asked for it: "Please, Lord . . . grant me."

Nehemiah offered his last-minute request to God after four months of fervent prayer. He knew that God had called him to this special work. He had sought counsel, planned as much as he could, anticipated questions, and waited patiently for God's timing. He had done everything he could do. His PowerPoint presentation was compelling and spell-checked. His associates were encouraging him with "Go get 'em; you're ready; you can do it." He knew he was a favorite of the king. He had every reason to be confident, yet his prayer was not "I've earned this" or "You owe me," it was "Grant me." Ever humble, Nehemiah knew that proudly strutting into either God's presence or the king's was not the path of favor. It's still not.

Do you remember how Jim Collins described Level 5 leaders in *Good to Great?* They are "modest and willful, humble and fearless." Best-selling business author Patrick Lencioni offers his version of the same idea in *Getting Naked*: "It is ultimately our honesty, humility, and selflessness that will endear us."[37] The Bible says it this way: "God opposes the proud, but favors the humble" (James 4:6 NLT). One of the prerequisites for favor with God and man is humility. It is the starting point for favor, but it's not enough. Most kings, CEOs, managers, and lead pastors expect more—a lot more.

FAVOR WITH MAN

Nehemiah prayed for *specific* favor, not for general favor. He already had that. How do I know? Because of the last phrase of Nehemiah 1:11: "I was cupbearer to the king."

The cupbearer's job was a lot bigger than sipping the king's wine to make sure it wasn't poisoned. If that was all there was to it, they could have grabbed the nearest slave and said, "Here, drink this." If the slave smacked his lips and said, "Yummy," he would get to go back to the dungeon or brickyard. If he gasped and fell over dead, everyone who had been within five miles of the wine cellar in the past month would be executed. Titles that we would use today for Nehemiah's position are Chief Steward, Chief Butler, maybe even Chief of Staff.

The cupbearer was in the presence of the king every day. No one without the king's (general) favor could serve in that role. It was not an "anybody will do" position. As the *Tyndale Concise Bible Commentary* notes:

> As the king's "cup-bearer" . . . he held a position of great responsibility and influence in the Persian court. Not only did he drink first of the king's wine to guard against poisoning, but he also kept accounts and exercised other administrative responsibilities. Only a person of exceptional trustworthiness would be given such a post.[38]

"Exceptional trustworthiness" and exceptional skill were part of the cupbearer's job description, and because King Artaxerxes was an absolute monarch, the slightest glitch could mean demotion to scrubbing pots in the kitchen, if not hanging from the gallows. There was no human resources department to appeal to. It was either earn the king's favor every day and keep the job, or fall out of favor and head for the kitchen . . . if you were lucky. How did Nehemiah earn the king's favor? The same way we earn favor today—by being exceptional: "Do you see a man skilled in his work? He will stand in the presence of kings" (Proverbs 22:29 HCSB).

Nehemiah served Artaxerxes every day, not because he was some court official's son or daughter (he was a Jew and a slave), but because he was exceptional. As Nehemiah's story unfolds, we will see that before he became an exceptional leader, he was an exceptional servant. If he were not, he would never have been cupbearer to the king.

In my various leadership roles, I have been blessed to have exceptional people serve and support me. They earned favor with me. When they needed a hearing to ask for special favor, they got the hearing, and more often than not, they got a "yes" to their requests. They were all different in their talents and personalities, but they all had these things in common:

- They were trustworthy. They did what they said they would do whether it was a huge project that took months (install a new $4 million management information system before midnight on December 31, 2000), something simple (set up a meeting with the union officers at 3:00 p.m. tomorrow), or something hard (call corporate to explain why we will miss our cash plan this month and won't be back on plan until the fourth quarter).

- They were not high maintenance. I didn't dread it when they walked into my office. They didn't expect me to be their counselor or therapist, and they didn't expect me to fix all their problems.

- They were focused on the company's needs, not personal agendas. They knew that promotions would come if they excelled in the job they had rather than worrying about the job they wanted.

- They were positive and fun to work with. I looked forward to time with them. They didn't bring gloominess into the room when they entered.

- They got results. They knew that working hard and being lovable was not the goal. We needed to satisfy customers, deliver profits, motivate and develop employees, and introduce new products.

■■ They told me the truth when I messed up. There was no sugar coating or walking on egg shells around the boss. They believed Solomon was right when he said, "He who rebukes a man will in the end gain more favor than he who has a flattering tongue (Proverbs 28:23 NIV).

■■ They gained my favor without manipulating, maneuvering, flattering, politicking, or abusing others. They had a simple strategy: be exceptional every day. It worked for them. It worked for Nehemiah. It will work for you.

Leadership STONE 4 THE MOST IMPORTANT JOB YOU'LL EVER HAVE IS THE JOB YOU HAVE NOW.

In chapter 3, we observed Nehemiah as he spent four long months in the waiting room. He made good use of the time, praying and planning. He spent hours before God asking Him to move the stones only God could move. He wore out Hanani with questions while he did as much planning as possible before asking permission for his trip to Jerusalem. He didn't jump the gun, but waited patiently for the right time, knowing he would get only one chance with the king. And though his heart and mind were already in Jerusalem rebuilding the wall, his body was stuck in Susa serving as the king's cupbearer. Sound familiar . . . stuck in one job when you want to be in another? How did you handle it? Did you hate going to work and slack off, or did you, like Nehemiah, realize that *the most important job you'll ever have is the job you have now* and continue to perform with diligence and excellence, giving your best every day?

Visualize for a moment a scenario in which Nehemiah let Jerusalem distract him from doing his best as cupbearer. When he entered the king's chamber, his mind was elsewhere, and he seemed uninterested in the task at hand, or worse, resentful and depressed. Because he was inattentive, the kitchen staff made mistakes: the mashed potatoes were lumpy and the quail undercooked and cold. When asked about it, Nehemiah made some lame excuse or offered an insincere, "It won't happen again." But it did happen again . . . and again.

How many "overs" do you get with a king? Not many. Certainly not four months' worth. There is no doubt that Nehemiah did not let his preoccupation with Jerusalem affect his performance as cupbearer. It wasn't easy, but the same excellence that elevated him to cupbearer in the first place sustained him as cupbearer even though he was emotionally ready to move on. Remember that he needed the king's favor for two reasons: first, to get a chance even to make his request; second, to get "yes" as an answer. The second favor he was asking God to grant him; the first he had to earn.

Now some of you are thinking that God could grant him both. Yes, He could, but would He? How often have you seen God intervene to grant favor to someone whose work is lazy, sloppy, grudging, and mediocre? I've never seen it. It would be a violation of God's character and Word. Remember what He says about our work:

> Do you see a man skilled in his work? He will stand in the presence of kings. (Proverbs 22:29 HCSB)

> Diligent work gets a warm commendation. (Proverbs 14:35 *The Message*)

> Whatever your hands find to do, do with all your strength. (Ecclesiastes 9:10 HCSB)

> Whatever you do, do everything for God's glory. (1 Corinthians 10:31 HCSB)

Think you are ready for a promotion and more responsibility? Pay attention to what Jesus had to say: "'Well done, good slave!' he told him. 'Because you have been faithful in a very small matter, have authority over 10 towns'" (Luke 19:17 HCSB).

Want to get unstuck from a dead-end or unsatisfying job? Whether you are in business or ministry, *step it up where you are.*

Do you view your current situation as preparation for the future even if it feels more like drudgery or punishment?

Are you bringing excellence to your job every day even if you don't enjoy it?

What about your attitude? Are you complaining, negative, or passive? Are you expecting a promotion with that kind of attitude?

Is it possible God is using your current position to shape and prepare you for some unseen new challenge a few years from now?

Could you answer the question "Why should I promote you?" with something more convincing than "I have been here a long time"?

Are you focused on serving and delivering results in the job you have now?

Remember that the most important job you'll ever have is the job you have, not the job you want. You have to *serve* with excellence before you can *lead* with excellence. ■

5

GAME DAY

Everyone has his own specific vocation or mission in life;
everyone must carry out a concrete assignment that demands fulfillment.
Therein he cannot be replaced, nor can his life be repeated, thus,
everyone's task is unique as is his specific
opportunity to implement it.[39]

VIKTOR E. FRANKL

Nehemiah was a nervous wreck this morning. We had breakfast together . . . sort of. He just picked at his food, not eating much of anything. When I asked if he was sick, he just said, "No." That's all. So I asked if there's trouble in the kitchen. "No" again. He was being so tight-lipped that I played the "brother" card: "I'm your brother, Nehemiah. For crying out loud, what's wrong?"

His answer surprised me: "I think today is the day. I'm going to get a chance to talk to the king about Jerusalem, and I'm scared."

Now I understand. This could be the greatest day of Nehemiah's life—or the worst. Everything depends on what kind of mood the king is in. If Nehemiah does get to raise the subject, he could hear either "How dare you! You're fired!" or "Get back in the kitchen, and keep your mind on your job." No wonder he's scared.

When I asked why he thought today would be the day, he said, "I'm not sure. I just sense it in my spirit."

Hmmm. After his four months of praying and planning, I'm wondering if that means Nehemiah has heard from God. Even if he has, talking to the king will still take a lot of courage. Throne room protocol is "don't speak unless spoken to." Will Nehemiah dare bring the subject up, or is it possible the king will? Wow, wouldn't that be something! Only God can make that happen.

NEHEMIAH'S JOURNAL

"In the month of Nisan in the twentieth year of King Artaxerxes, when wine was brought for him, I took the wine and gave it to the king. I had not been sad in his presence before; so the king asked me, 'Why does your face look so sad when you are not ill? This can be nothing but sadness of heart.' I was very much afraid, but I said to the king, 'May the king live forever! Why should my face not look sad when the city where my fathers are buried lies in ruins, and its gates have been destroyed by fire?' The king said to me, 'What is it you want?' Then I prayed to the God of heaven, and I answered the king, 'If it pleases the king and if your servant has found favor in his sight, let him send me to the city in Judah where my fathers are buried so that I can rebuild it.'

"Then the king, with the queen sitting beside him, asked me, 'How long will your journey take, and when will you get back?' It pleased the king to send me; so I set a time. I also said to him, 'If it pleases the king, may I have letters to the governors of Trans-Euphrates, so that they will provide me safe-conduct until I arrive in Judah? And may I have a letter to Asaph, keeper of the king's forest, so he will give me timber to make beams for the gates of the citadel by the temple and for the city wall and for the residence I will occupy?' And because the gracious hand of my God was upon me, the king granted my requests. So I went to the governors of Trans-Euphrates and gave them the king's letters. The king had also sent army officers and cavalry with me." (Nehemiah 2:1–9 NIV)

THE YELLOW BRICK ROAD

I have seen the movie 127 times, never missing it for about ten years as my two daughters begged, "Daddy, please watch *The Wizard of Oz* with us. Please! Please!"

Because they did not often hear "no" from me as they grew up (they still don't), I would plop down on the floor with them and pretend to be enthralled by it one more time. Not infrequently I would hear, "Daddy, Daddy, wake up, you're missing the best part."

If you have children, you know the *Oz* plot as well as I do.[40] The four main characters—Dorothy, the Scarecrow, the Tin Woodman, and the Cowardly Lion—all need something that they can get only from the Wizard who resides in Emerald City at the end of the yellow brick road. Dorothy wants to go home to Kansas; the Scarecrow needs a brain; the Tin Woodman yearns for a heart; the Cowardly Lion hopes for courage.

After days of perilous travel down the yellow thoroughfare, the four arrive at the Emerald City, excited to see the Wizard, whom they believe will give them everything they ask for. At least they are all excited except the Cowardly Lion, who has a panic attack as they walk into the Wizard's foyer. The dialog goes like this:

Cowardly Lion—"Wait a minute, fellows. I was just thinking. I really don't want to see the Wizard this much. I'd better wait for you outside."

Scarecrow—"What's the matter?"

Tin Woodman—"Oh, he's just scared again."

Dorothy—"Don't you know the Wizard's going to give you some courage?"

Cowardly Lion—"I'd be too scared to ask him for it."

Dorothy—"Well then, we'll ask him for you."

Cowardly Lion—"I'd sooner wait outside."

Dorothy—"Why? Why?"

Cowardly Lion—"Because I'm still scared."

Does "I'd be too scared to ask him for it" ring a bell? You've been there, haven't you? I have. *Every* leader is there from time to time. I have been to the CEO's office to ask for $100 million to invest in a new product. My knees were knocking. Months of planning and hundreds of jobs were on the line. Everyone back home was counting on me, but the truth was, it was all up to the CEO. Would he be in a "yes" mood ("Let's support those guys in Nashville!") or in a "no" state of mind ("Forget it. We've got other fish to fry.")? Sound familiar? Maybe it was the elder board at your church, or your manager, or your spouse. Whatever it was and whoever you had to ask, the outcome was out of your hands. There was nothing more you could do except breathe a prayer, calm your nerves, then walk through the door into the office . . . or conference room . . . or auditorium . . . or throne room, with courage. That's what Nehemiah had to do. It was game day for Nehemiah. It was time to "fish or cut bait." He was at the end of the yellow brick road and had to choose whether to hang out in the foyer, or courageously ("I was very much afraid"—Nehemiah 2:2 NIV) enter the throne room to ask for what he wanted. After all, leaders can't pray and plan forever. At some point they have to move out.

BUTTERFLIES

Butterflies in the stomach are common. Junior high boys get them when Brittney walks by and smiles. High school seniors get them when *The Letter* from *The College* arrives. Few things cause more butterflies than meeting *The Parents* for the first time. (My future mother-in-law's reaction was, "At least he doesn't have long hair.") Geeks get them while standing in line at the Apple Store waiting for the new iWhatever. My older daughter, Elizabeth, in spite of taking the stage hundreds of times, still gets butterflies, especially on opening night. Athletes get them on game day (even if their name is Michael or Peyton or Tiger). Many leaders have a pack of TUMS in their top drawer to quiet the butterflies they experience before an important meeting with *The Board*, or a potential big customer, or every pastor's nightmare—*The Deacon Body*.

The Cowardly Lion was trapped in a classic catch-22: he needed to see the Wizard to gain courage, but he didn't have enough courage to see the Wizard. Until he overcame his fear, he couldn't get what he wanted and needed. The Cowardly Lion was confused. He thought that if he was afraid, it meant he didn't have courage. He had to learn that courage means acting *in spite of* fear, and so do we all—especially when we are in a leadership role. We can pray and plan for months, but when game day comes, so will the flutters. They did for Nehemiah, and why not? After all, he was taking a big risk: "A king's terrible wrath is like the roaring of a lion; anyone who provokes him endangers himself" (Proverbs 20:2 HCSB).

On Nehemiah's game day, he was serving wine to the king. The very best thing that could have happened was the king saying something like this: "Nehemiah, I've been thinking that it's time to rebuild the walls of Jerusalem. The city is defenseless, and if the Egyptians attack, we couldn't hold it. How would you like to go to Jerusalem as the construction manager to oversee the project? Better yet, I'll appoint you as governor of all of Judah. How does that sound? Are you interested?"

Well, that didn't happen, but the second best thing *did*. The king gave Nehemiah permission to speak when he asked, "Why does your face look so sad when you are not ill? This can be nothing but sadness of heart" (Nehemiah 2:2 NIV). Wow! With one simple question, the king poured out favor on Nehemiah in three ways: (1) The king showed he was concerned about Nehemiah; he really was the king's favorite (chapter 4). (2) Nehemiah wasn't going to be thrown out of the king's chamber for being sad. (The king's favorite song was *Smiling Happy People* by the fifth century BC version of R.E.M. Look it up on Wikipedia if you don't know.) (3) Nehemiah was given permission to speak without even asking.

The king opened the door wide for Nehemiah. However, Nehemiah, being much like us (or at least like me), was still "very much afraid." He had butterflies to overcome. He could take the easy way out with, "I'm fine, just a little sad because my brother is leaving in a couple of days." Or he could summon his courage, breathe one last prayer—which he did—and ask the king for permission to go to Jerusalem to rebuild the walls.

"YOU WANT TO DO *WHAT?*"

Thomas Edison once said, "Good fortune is what happens when opportunity meets with planning."[41] Because Nehemiah did not waste the wait, he had a lot more going for him than opportunity and planning. He had four months of prayer supporting him. He was as prepared as he could be without actually seeing the walls. He had a strong sense of God's calling. He had earned the favor of the king through diligent, excellent service. And on game day, the king made it easy for him to raise the subject.

But Nehemiah could still blow it. The king handed Nehemiah the ball, and he had to run with it. He could miss the handoff, fumble, or stumble. Or if you prefer a non-athletic metaphor: he could be off-key or hit the wrong chord, hurting the king's ears. The door is open, but he doesn't have "yes" yet.

Getting to YES is a long-term, best-selling book (more than 10 million copies in more than thirty languages) first published in 1981. The subtitle is *Negotiating Agreement Without Giving In.* In spite of the subtitle, this useful book is actually intended to lead to what we today call "win-win" outcomes. As Nehemiah entered the king's chamber, he didn't have a copy of *Getting to YES,* and it wouldn't have helped if he did. Why? Because kings don't negotiate with their servants. Nehemiah had to use a different approach, one that is a great leadership case study on how to approach a king, CEO, manager, or senior pastor with what seems to be an outlandish request. We can learn a lot from examining how Nehemiah petitioned the king:

- **He was respectful**—"May the king live forever" and "If it pleases the king . . . ." He honored the king's position, making it clear that he was asking, not demanding. There is no better example in all the Bible of Proverbs 22:11 in action: "He . . . whose speech is gracious will have the king for his friend" (NIV).

- **He was honest**—"Why should my face not look sad when the city where my fathers are buried lies in ruins, and its gates have been destroyed by fire?" He didn't skirt the issue. He was open and aboveboard. Importantly, he answered the exact question the king asked.

- **He was clear, concise, and specific**—" . . . send me to the city in Judah where my fathers are buried so that I can rebuild it." Kings, CEOs, managers, and others in positions of authority are busy. They don't have all day to listen to a rambling request. The best communication is always clear (simple, unambiguous), concise (few words, to the point), and specific (defining exactly what the request is).

- **He was prepared**—"Then the king, with the queen sitting beside him, asked me, 'How long will your journey take, and when will you get back?' It pleased the king to send me; so I set a time." Remember chapter 3? Nehemiah had anticipated questions and was ready with answers.

■■ **He was unselfish**—"The city where my fathers are buried lies in ruins, and its gates have been destroyed by fire." There was not one self-centered thing about Nehemiah's request.

The king could easily have been incredulous: "You want to do *what?*" Instead, "it pleased the king to send me" (Nehemiah 2:6 NIV). Actually, Nehemiah got more than he asked for: "The king . . . also sent army officers and cavalry with me" (Nehemiah 2:9 NIV). Not a bad outcome for a cupbearer who entered the king's chamber when "very much afraid."

Leadership STONE 5 COURAGE TO ACT

Three things await leaders on game day. First, the time of preparation is over. It is the end of the yellow brick road, time to take the field, fish or cut bait, pick up the guitar and play. Second, the butterflies swarm. If the stakes are high—and they often are for leaders—butterflies almost always show up. Third, the answer, yes or no, is waiting for you. You either get the $100 million for the new product, or you don't. You get approval from the elders for a new worship center, or you don't. You get to go to Jerusalem, or you don't. It's no wonder leaders don't sleep well the night before game day and often throw up in the morning.

I've had to face quite a few game days. Some had to do with my leadership roles in business or at church. Some were personal, like the game day for this book. I had talked about it for years but had done nothing. A friend (thanks, Carl) called my hand: "Dick, when are you going to get over your fear of failure and start writing?"

I'm still afraid of failure, but I'm more afraid of having regrets for not trying. I think Nehemiah was in the same boat. He could overcome his fear and ask the king, knowing he might hear "no," or spend the rest of his life regretting that he didn't ask.

One of the things that makes leadership hard is that it takes courage. You can't lead without it. Sooner or later that outlandish thing you want to do—or God has called you to do—will require courage to act. You can pray and plan (and you should), but game day *will* come; you can't put it off forever. If you do put it off, you may carry the heavy mantle of regret for a long time.

Are you standing in the foyer trying to decide whether to go in or not? If so, remember:

> **Be strong and courageous! Do not be afraid . . . . For the Lord your God will personally go ahead of you. He will neither fail you nor abandon you. (Deuteronomy 31:6 NLT)**

> **And because the gracious hand of my God was upon me, the king granted my requests. (Nehemiah 2:8 NIV)**

Does fear of failure have you or your organization on the sidelines instead of in the game?

Will you have life-long regrets if you don't go for it—whatever "it" is?

Do you have a friend who will challenge you to go for it in spite of your fears? If you don't, find one. ●

6

THE HARDEST PERSON TO LEAD

The hardest person you will
ever have to lead is yourself."[42]

BILL GEORGE

We left Susa for Jerusalem a week after the king appointed Nehemiah as governor of Judah (wow!) and approved rebuilding the wall. Talk about more than we had even hoped for!

Since we had twenty camels carrying extra water, we took the short route straight across the desert. As always, it was a hot and dry journey, but we made it in record time.

The Jordan River was a sight for sore eyes—we crossed it yesterday. We stopped long enough to bathe (along with a lot of splashing, joking, and laughing). It was the first time I'd been cool since we left the palace weeks ago. We were all anxious to get home to our families. Nehemiah wanted to leave early the next morning so we could get there before dark, but that didn't work out. Just about the time we got the camels loaded and ready to go, a greeting party from Jerusalem showed up: Eliashib, the high priest, along with Rephaiah and Shallum, both important officials in Jerusalem. They wanted to extend an official welcome and let Nehemiah know what was planned for his arrival. He listened quietly as they told him their agenda for his first three days in Jerusalem. First, a welcoming banquet for about 300 people—all the movers and shakers in Jerusalem and the surrounding towns. Second, a visit to the temple, hosted by Eliashib, with special sacrifices planned to ensure God's blessing on Nehemiah's reign as governor. (I still can't believe he's actually going to be governor!) Third, a tour of the city led by Rephaiah and Shallum so they can brief him on what needs to be done. Finally, a huge parade down King David Way to give all the people a chance to see and cheer Nehemiah. Evidently, they've spent days preparing and want to make a good impression.

Nehemiah's response caught me off guard. "Thank you," he said, "but please cancel everything. I'm not here to reign. I'm here to serve. I do want to meet the people, but first I'd like a couple of days to rest and look around on my own."

I couldn't tell if they were disappointed or impressed. Most new governors would want to make a big splash when they arrive and would revel in parades and banquets. Not Nehemiah. He's obviously going to be a different kind of governor than we've had in the past. I wonder if the people will like that. And wanting to rest? Sure, the trip was hard, but I thought he would want to hit the ground running. Oh well, I doubt if this will be the last surprise he has for us.

NEHEMIAH'S JOURNAL

"I went to Jerusalem, and after staying there three days, I set out during the night with a few men." (Nehemiah 2:11-12 NIV)

⠿ ⠿ ⠿ ⠿

LEAD YOURSELF FIRST

According to Nehemiah 2:11, after Nehemiah arrived in Jerusalem, he went underground for three days. Let me admit that I am going to speculate a bit here. However, it is not wild speculation; it is based on what we know about Nehemiah's character and personality. I think we can say with confidence that those three days were spent resting and praying, restoring his body and refreshing his spirit.

Bill Hybels, in *Courageous Leadership*, calls self-leadership our "toughest leadership challenge."[43]

Make no mistake about it: if you can't lead yourself, you won't be able to effectively lead others. You might be able to *boss* others, but you won't be able to lead them. The most effective leaders are healthy in every dimension of life—body, soul, and spirit. They take intentional steps to get healthy and stay healthy. So I don't think it is too much of a stretch to believe that Nehemiah's first order of business was to take care of himself so he would have the physical, emotional, and spiritual strength needed for the hard task of leadership that lay ahead of him.

REST

A few years ago, we took a family vacation to Disney World. It was great! My three grandsons enjoyed every minute of the adventure. The Magic Kingdom was truly magic for them, and the Animal Kingdom was much better than a trip to the local zoo. We have dozens of pictures: Aaron with Goofy, Caleb with Mickey Mouse, and a wide-eyed Seth (only nine months old at the time) taking it all in from his stroller. We returned home with lots of memories and a vow to go back when Seth is older. It was a terrific trip, but it wasn't rest. It was typical of so many vacations that prompt us to say, "I need a vacation to recover from my vacation."

God didn't waste much time before He let us know how important rest is by making it a page-one headline. In only the thirty-third verse of the Bible (Genesis 2:2), it says that on the seventh day God (Himself!) rested from all His work: "He rested on the seventh day from all the work which He had done" (Genesis 2:2 NASB). That may seem a bit curious because later (Isaiah 40:28) the Bible says God doesn't get tired. So why did He rest if He wasn't tired? He did it as an example to us because we *do* get tired and need rest. If God took a break from His work, so should we.

Every leader—especially those in high-stress roles—needs rest, a break from the rigors of leading. No calls from the office. No checking email. No CNBC or *Wall Street Journal*. I know, some of you are thinking, "Impossible, my company (or department or church or whatever) couldn't make it for a week without me." I used to think that, too. The truth is, that kind of thinking is an affront to God because it is fed by arrogance ("They can't do without me" and "I know what I need better than God does"). It is also flatly disobedient to His Word which says we ought to take a break from our work at least one day every single week: "You have six days each week for your ordinary work, but the seventh day is a Sabbath day of rest . . . . On that day no one . . . may do any work" (Exodus 20:9–10 NLT).

Are you thinking, "No way; He can't be serious"? I suspect that is what the Israelites thought when Moses first passed on the "day of rest" commandment. They were primarily farmers and shepherds—seven-day-a-week jobs to be sure. So later in Exodus, God emphasizes how serious He is about rest when He says to the farmers, "You are to labor six days but you must rest on the seventh day; you must even rest during plowing and harvesting times" (Exodus 34:21 HCSB).

Even "during plowing and harvesting times"! In an agricultural economy, plowing and harvesting times are the busiest times of the year. Is God saying it's a "good idea" to rest even during the busiest time of the year? NO! He said, "You *must* rest" during the busiest times of the year. CPA, even during tax season you must rest. Retailer, even during December you must rest. Coach, even during football season you must rest. Pastor, even during a building program you must rest. CEO, even when preparing for the annual shareholders meeting you must rest. Dick, even when writing a book you must rest. (Yesterday was Sunday. I went to church, took a nap, had dinner with my grandsons, and capped off the day watching an old movie. It was a great break.)

If you think the farmers were stunned by "you must rest" during harvest time, imagine how they felt about God's command that every seven years the land should be left untilled for a full year: "Plant and harvest your crops for six years, but let the land be renewed and lie uncultivated during the seventh year" (Exodus 23:10–11 NLT). What? Every seven years abandon the fields to weeds and mice? That's what He said. In other words, in the same way you'll be more productive in six days if you rest on the seventh, your land will be more productive in six years if it rests the seventh year. By this, God introduced the concept of extended rest, or what I call *escape*.

ESCAPE

I have found, at least for me, fully restorative rest only comes with escape. My body, soul, and spirit all need occasional escape from the everyday world. For years my escape has been either the North Georgia mountains or the coast of Downeast Maine—a week of nothing but coffee, a good book or two, eating catfish or lobster, and listening to the creek or watching the waves. There is no doubt in my mind that without escape, the stress of running a midsize company or later serving a large church would have produced what Bill Hybels calls "many broken pieces rattling around inside me."[44] For Hybels, escape is on his sailboat. He says in *Courageous Leadership*, "I shudder to think where I'd be today had I not given myself permission to take up boating again."[45]

One mistake we make is equating *different* with *escape*. Let me clarify: taking your office to a different place is not escape. An open briefcase and ringing Blackberry at the beach is different, but it is not escape. Senior pastor, you can round up a couple of pastor buddies, play eighteen holes and then have dinner, all the while talking about your church problems. That is different, but it's not escape. Business leader, you can take your team to the Willow Creek Leadership Summit (which I highly recommend) to be inspired and challenged. That is different and worthwhile, but it is not escape. Escape is leaving it all behind, emptying your mind of your ordinary work as Exodus 20:9 calls it, and letting God repair and refresh you from head to foot. In my own experience, I have found that I can get physical rest in a couple of days; however, mental and emotional rest usually takes a week or more.

You need to escape, but *who* you escape with is also important. My wife, Dottie, is wired much like I am. She doesn't need to be entertained; she doesn't have to be sightseeing all the time; she doesn't need to be talking all the time; a day of nothing but sitting on the porch with a good book or working a puzzle is fine with her. She is a great escape partner. Once a year, I spend a couple of days alone intensely seeking God, but most of the time, I escape with her. My point is, choose your escape partner carefully. Remember, the purpose of escape is to detox from the stresses of your ordinary life, not just drag them to a different place.

OX IN THE PIT

In Luke 14:15, Jesus makes it clear that if your ox falls in a pit, it is okay to pull it out on the Sabbath. He didn't say that "just because you are extra busy" it's okay to give up your day of rest. (Remember, I pointed out earlier that God said we should rest even during the busiest time of the year.) He was saying that "when you have a crisis" it is okay to work on your day of rest. An ox in a pit was a true crisis for a farmer in Jesus' day. It's a little harder to decide what a twenty-first-century crisis is in our complex global economy. So I am going to leave it up to you, grappling with God, to define your personal ox-in-the-pit situations. However, here are three ox-in-the-pit things to think about:

- The ox in the pit is supposed to be an occasional, temporary situation, not the running commentary of your work life. If you are using the ox in the pit as a week-after-week excuse, then you have missed Jesus' point entirely and are flatly disobedient to God's command that we are to rest on a weekly basis.

- If your ox is truly in the pit most of the time, and if you are a senior leader in your organization (company, department, church, etc.), then you need to step up your leadership, get the ox out of the pit, and keep it out. It is your job, your responsibility, not someone else's.

- If your organization's ox is in the pit all the time, and you are not in a position of leadership that can help get it out, you need to consider whether moving to a new situation is the right thing for you. It will be hard for you to be physically, emotionally, and spiritually healthy if you are working in a never-ending ox-in-the-pit environment.

THREE SUGGESTIONS

#1—Simplify. Back in the mid-1990s, Dottie once announced to me, "Our life is berserk." What she really meant was, "Your berserk life is making mine berserk."

She was right. I was traveling more than 100,000 miles per year on business, was serving on the Board of the Nashville Chamber of Commerce, was the chairman of a technology taskforce for Nashville schools, and was trying to fill three roles at my church including leading a building program. I had what I called a "zero free time" life, and frankly, I was proud of it: *If all these people want my help, I must be the only one who can do the job. It's nice to have the mayor and future governor asking me to do something for him, and being interviewed on TV is kind of cool.*

The hard truth is, my ego was out of control, and that was driving my schedule out of control. I have always been grateful that Dottie called me on it. It took about a year to simplify my life and to learn that "no" is a perfectly good English word that needed to be in my vocabulary.

There are at least four things at risk when we pile more on our plate than we can handle:

- We risk physical and emotional burnout, even to the point of becoming nonfunctional.
- We risk performing with mediocrity instead of excellence. (The mayor or governor doesn't call hoping for mediocre help.)
- We risk making mistakes; balls get dropped, and instead of helping, damage is done.
- We risk damaged relationships—family, friends, or coworkers become victims.

Need some physical and emotional rest? *Simplify your life.* Do it by using what Bill Hybels calls the leader's "powerful NO muscle"[46]—say "no" more often—you'll learn to like it.

#2—Take care of your body. I won't dwell on the lifestyle we all need to have healthy bodies. Go to your local bookstore, and you will find all you need to know in the rows and rows of books on diet and exercise. If you are news-aware at all, you know about the obesity pandemic in America that arises from too many cheeseburgers and french fries and too much time in front of the flat screen with a remote control in our hands. Let me simply make three observations from my own experience:

- My (and your) body, mind, soul, and spirit are interrelated and work together. When any one of them is out of order, it affects the others. When I feel bad physically, I am cranky or reclusive. When I am emotionally down, I have no desire to exercise, but when I do exercise, my emotions are lifted. When my weight is up, I feel sluggish, less alert, and don't rest well. So to be on top of my game, I have to take care of "all of me"— body, mind, soul, and spirit.
- During those times when I take care of my body by healthier eating and consistent exercise, I am a much more effective leader. I am mentally sharper and handle stress much better. There is no doubt that when I feel better physically, I lead better. You will, too.
- More often than not, the most effective senior-level leaders— consistently leading at a high level on a long-term basis—are physically fit. They make regular visits to the exercise room and the salad bar. If you aren't sure about this, watch your favorite TV business channel for a week, taking special note of the

evident physical fitness of the C-level executives. I think you'll be surprised.

I am not trying to make you feel guilty about this. I am simply saying there is a strong connection between our ability to lead well—especially over the long haul—and our physical health. Though there are physiologic and genetic factors that influence our health, for most of us, the number one factor is just good old-fashioned self-discipline. In *True North*, Bill George says that the most successful authentic leaders have "a consistently high level of self-discipline . . . . reflected in their personal lives as well, because without personal self-discipline it is not possible to sustain self-discipline at work."[47]

Note that he did not say we couldn't have short bursts of self-discipline at work. He said we couldn't *sustain* it. Conventional wisdom says it takes at least twenty-one days to form a habit but only one day to break it. Is it possible that's why so many leaders are like a yo-yo: up . . . down . . . up . . . down . . . up . . . down, until the string finally breaks or becomes a tangled mess? Self-discipline is hard. Admittedly, I have a spotty track record. But I know the truth, and I am without excuse. How about you?

#3—Get help. In *Courageous Leadership*, Bill Hybels makes two great points about self-leadership, which I summarize this way:

- It is the leader's personal responsibility. It is not someone else's job. Quit blaming others and take the reins and do the hard job of leading yourself.
- Get help if you need it.

Help can be a professional counselor, an accountability partner or group, a trainer, a nutritionist, or someone else to whom you can hold yourself responsible. The point is, you are more likely to be successful if you don't "go it alone."

Leaders, especially high-profile senior leaders—and particularly pastors—are fearfully reluctant to seek help. It is partly pride but also concern about what people will say—and they *will* say something. They did about Hybels. However, he considered the risk of rumors less than the risk of continuing without help. In fact, he says, "I knew there was no way I could continue."[48] If Hybels, the senior pastor and leader of one of the largest and most influential ministries in America, is willing to admit the need for help, so can I, and so can you. Wouldn't you rather deal with the rumors than with the headlines that follow a major breakdown in your life?

DON'T IGNORE . . .

Your Emotional Health. This is a complex subject beyond the level of my expertise, but I know it is crucial to effective leadership. Your ability to lead will be greatly diminished—even destroyed—if your emotions are high one minute, depressed the next; if anger resides shallowly within you and frequently erupts out of control; if you are constantly worrying about your finances; if fragile or broken relationships are constantly on your mind. Leaders in this state are often quick to blame others for their emotional dysfunction. But the truth is, whether you are in business or ministry, your emotional health is *your* responsibility. Only you can take the steps that will lead you out of the storm into the calm—steps like the ones outlined below.

#1—Release anger. It has been my observation that close-to-the-surface anger that too often strikes out in rage at others is almost always the result of bitterness residing in an unforgiving heart. In *Unbroken*, Laura Hillenbrand's remarkable telling of Louis Zamperini's story, she says this about unforgiveness and desiring revenge:

> The paradox of vengefulness is that it makes men dependent upon those who have harmed them, believing that their release from pain will come only when they make their tormentors suffer. In seeking the Bird's death to free himself, Louie had chained himself, once again, to his tyrant. During the war, the Bird had been unwilling to let go of Louie; after the war, Louie was unable to let go of the Bird.[49]

In his letter to the church at Ephesus, Paul challenges us to remove bitterness, anger, and wrath and to extend forgiveness to those who have hurt us:

> All bitterness, anger and wrath, insult and slander must be removed from you, along with all wickedness. And be kind and compassionate to one another, forgiving one another, just as God also forgave you in Christ. (Ephesians 4:31–32 HCSB)

This is a matter of utmost spiritual importance, but it is also a matter of utmost practical importance to leadership. Easily angered leaders produce a climate of fear that buries the truth and crushes the spirit of an organization.

If anger is one of your leadership tools, then please don't ignore my plea—get help. Don't let anger and unforgiveness destroy your leadership credibility. The cost is too high—to you personally and to your organization.

#2—Get out of debt. Debt is a four-letter word, a ball-and-chain you have to drag around all the time. It is exhausting. It destroys relationships. It will affect your productivity. It will damage your effectiveness as a leader. And worse, when personal finances begin to consume and overwhelm you, the desperate need for relief can plant ideas in your head you never thought possible. As Benjamin Disraeli once said, "Debt is a prolific mother of folly and crime."[50]

Why are "folly and crime" so easily birthed by debt? Because "the borrower is a slave to the lender" (Proverbs 22:7 HCSB). It is as simple as this: you cannot lead yourself well and be emotionally healthy when you are burdened by debt, not to mention that it is disobedience to God's Word. This is another one of those "self-discipline" issues. Who is responsible? You are. Not sure how to get started? Financial Peace University has great resources (www.daveramsey.com/fpu) that will help you develop a plan and encourage you to stick with it.

#3—Heal relationships. About a year ago, one of my great failures in leadership and relationships was exposed when a former coworker (I had been his supervisor) said over a cup of coffee, "Dick, I want you to know I have forgiven you." This was a man I truly cared for, but because he had an "easygoing" personality, he had been the target of my teasing and pranks on too many occasions. Even as I write these words, I am ashamed that he took the initiative to extend forgiveness when I should have taken the initiative to seek forgiveness. Don't make the same mistake. Heed the dictates of Scripture:

Make every effort to live in peace with all men. (Hebrews 12:14 NIV)

If it is possible, as far as it depends on you, live at peace with everyone. (Romans 12:18 NIV)

When leaders—especially Christian leaders—take the initiative to heal and strengthen relations, not only will their leadership be more effective, but that elusive thing we all seek called peace can be obtained.

Emotional health is definitely a "get help" area of life. Emotional dysfunction can arise from deep-seated, little understood, years-ago life events that can seldom be resolved by a cup of coffee with a friend or by reading the latest popular book. As you read this, you know if you need help. You may even have sought help in the past, but don't give up. Try again. Nothing is truer than "if you don't change direction, you'll end up where you're headed." Get help before it's too late. Do it for yourself, for your family, and for your organization.

Leadership STONE 6 | LEAD YOURSELF SO YOU WILL BE FIT TO LEAD OTHERS.

Nehemiah was getting ready to begin the biggest leadership challenge of his life. He knew he needed to rest and replenish his body, soul, and spirit. So what did he do? He shut down for three days. Sometimes three days of physical rest is exactly what we need. Other times we need more. We need emotional rest as well, and if we don't get it, we risk a lot of broken pieces rattling around inside ourselves.

Are you shutting down your "ordinary work" on a regular basis?

When was the last time you "left it all behind" for a week or more?

Are you making the mistake of assuming *different* is as effective as *rest* and *escape*?

Is your life berserk? What are you doing about it?

Are diet, weight, and exercise sensitive subjects to you? Why?

Are you an emotional basket case? Would your family or coworkers agree with your answer?

Will you commit today to take personal responsibility for your fitness to lead?

Will you get help if you need it? ◼

7

NO PARADES OR POWERPOINT

We're going dark for a bit while we assess the task at hand.[51]

LOUIS V. GERSTNER JR.

Nehemiah has spent the last three days mostly by himself. He's taken an early morning walk to the temple every day, but otherwise he's stayed alone in his tent just outside the city. He wouldn't meet with any of the city officials even though they asked repeatedly for time with him. I tried to smooth things over by promising he would meet with them in the "next day or so." The people in the city were also restless, wondering when he was going to show his face and do something. Frankly, I was wondering myself and was tired of answering their questions with "soon," hoping that the "next day or so" really would be the next day or so.

Finally, at about 3:00 this afternoon, Nehemiah came out of his tent and asked me to plan a tour of the wall after dark tonight. I asked if he wanted me to invite the city officials and reschedule the parade, but he said, "No parades. Just the two of us, along with Hananiah and a few guards." He wants to look at the situation for himself before he talks to anyone. Actually, he hasn't yet told anyone that he plans to rebuild the walls. The people probably think he's here as the new governor to make their lives more miserable by raising taxes and forcing them to build a big governor's palace. Why should they think otherwise? After all, that's what new governors usually do.

At last, "the next day or so" will be tomorrow. To follow up his wall tour tonight, he wants me to set a meeting with the city officials and chief priest tomorrow morning at 9:00, without telling them why. I bet there will be a lot of pacing-the-floor sleeplessness in Jerusalem tonight.

"After I arrived in Jerusalem and had been there three days, I got up at night and [took] a few men with me. I didn't tell anyone what my God had laid on my heart to do for Jerusalem. The only animal I took was the one I was riding. I went out at night through the Valley Gate toward the Serpent's Well and the Dung Gate, and I inspected the walls of Jerusalem that had been broken down and its gates that had been destroyed by fire. I went on to the Fountain Gate and the King's Pool, but farther down it became too narrow for my animal to go through. So I went up at night by way of the valley and inspected the wall. Then heading back, I entered through the Valley Gate and returned. The officials did not know where I had gone or what I was doing, for I had not yet told the Jews, priests, nobles, officials, or the rest of those who would be doing the work." (Nehemiah 2:11–16 HCSB)

:: :: :: ::

THERE'S A NEW SHERIFF IN TOWN

Based on verses 9 and 10 of Nehemiah 2, there is no doubt that the people of Jerusalem and the surrounding regions knew that Nehemiah was coming:

> So I went to the governors of Trans-Euphrates and gave them the king's letters. The king had also sent army officers and cavalry with me. When Sanballat the Horonite and Tobiah the Ammonite official heard about this, they were very much disturbed that someone had come to promote the welfare of the Israelites. (Nehemiah 2:9-10 NIV)

He had visited other governors on the route; he had an armed escort; even his enemies knew he was coming and "were very much disturbed." There was no way for him to sneak into town. Nehemiah's big arrival ceremony is described in chapter 2, verse 11: "After I arrived in Jerusalem and had been there three days . . . . " For three days he did nothing—at least nothing in public. No parades or receiving lines. No banquets. No arrival ceremony of any kind. He arrived . . . then disappeared . . . for three days. Imagine the watercooler scuttlebutt that caused!

The arrival of a new leader, any leader—sheriff, manager, owner, pastor, governor, or president—is a big deal. The employees, citizens, congregation, or whoever are both nervous and curious, with questions such as: "What does he look like?" "What will she do first?" "How is it going to affect me?" The more power the new leader has, the more nervous the people are.

The new leader's constituents always want to make a favorable first impression. Parades, banquets, presentations, and tours are a standard part of the "new sheriff in town" package. The new leader, too, often wants to make a favorable first impression and to quickly put his or her "fingerprints" on the organization, to make it "theirs."

I have experienced this new-sheriff syndrome from both sides. As a young engineer, I once made a fool of myself trying to impress a new VP of Engineering by telling him how much I hoped he would change everything, shake up the troops, and kick some rear ends. He wasn't impressed, and for the good of my own rear end, I exited the engineering department soon after that.

Later, at the same company, we got a new president, and of course, we all wondered what he would do first to put his fingerprints on the company. Maybe he would launch a major R&D project to ensure our future or initiate a company-wide reorganization to make us *lean and mean* to be more competitive. Surely, he would do *something* that would get everyone's attention in a big way. Nope. His first change was . . . to move the flag pole. Talk about shaking up the troops! That was huge (sarcasm admitted). Yet even though he didn't make a big-splash arrival, he was a thoughtful and effective leader for many years. (By the way, this time I did *not* make a fool of myself by telling him what he needed to do.)

I have also been the new leader, sitting through countless hours of listening to "how it really is": the designs are impossible to build, manufacturing is controlled by the union, plant supervisors think they know everything and never listen to the workers, finance doesn't care about anything but budgets, or the worship band is too loud. I made a lot of new-leader mistakes that I could have avoided by following Nehemiah's example. From Nehemiah

I have learned that the most important first decision a new leader makes is not about actions and rules; it is about tone. Every new leader sets a tone of either "You are a bunch of losers, and I'm here to save you" or "Working together we can be successful, and I'm here to help you."

I'M FROM CORPORATE AND I'M HERE TO SAVE YOU

New sheriffs do not always arrive because the walls are down and the organization is a wreck. Successful leaders (those who have the walls up and the organization thriving) have to be replaced because of retirements, promotions, and sometimes death. When Apple CEO Steve Jobs died in October 2011, Apple was one of the best run and highest value (based on stock price) companies in the world. His replacement, Tim Cook, was not tasked with *rebuilding* the company. His task was to sustain the excellence that was already there (very daunting, by the way), and he said so publicly in an email to the Apple staff on October 5, 2011, the day Jobs died: "We will honor his memory by dedicating ourselves to continuing the work he loved so much."

However, when new leaders are charged with a turnaround because the walls are down (profit, attendance, or whatever), they often arrive with a big splash and big announcements. After all, they have come on the scene to save an organization from the incompetence of the previous leader or the incompetence of the staff as a whole. The big announcements are usually made first in the main conference room to the management team. There is often a lot of maneuvering to influence the new leader—frequently a bunch of finger pointing. Not many people are willing to stand up and say, "I'm the problem." The new leader has to sort through all the input and decide what to do. Unfortunately, "ready, fire, aim" is a too-common approach because the new leader wants to be seen as decisive, dynamic, and dramatic: "The walls are down and drastic action is needed now!"

Nehemiah would be a big disappointment to the business press and Wall Street today. He made neither a big splash nor a big announcement. In fact, for the first three days, he said nothing:

I had not told anyone what my God had put in my heart to do for Jerusalem. (Nehemiah 2:12 NIV)

**As yet I had said nothing to the Jews or the priests or nobles or offi-
cials or any others. (Nehemiah 2:16 NIV)**

Imagine how that would go over today. He would be skewered. When
the walls are down, we expect new leaders to show up with solutions in hand
before they even know what the problems are. So what happens? In our rush
to raise earnings, increase donations, or boost attendance, we fix the symptoms but never get to the root cause of the problems. Like treating cancer
with aspirin, we reduce the deficit but don't eliminate it. We improve an old
product rather than introduce a new one. We change the style of music or
service starting times. We get short-term relief but not a long-term fix. The
symptoms soon reappear, and the talk begins again: "We aren't any better
off with the new guy than we were before."

A leader's job is not to make a big splash; it is to make a big difference. It is not to make a great first impression but a great lasting impression.
Nehemiah knew that how he *started* was not as important as how he would
finish. He did not buy into the "do something . . . anything" philosophy
of leadership. The walls had been down for more than 140 years. He knew
the only thing worse than doing nothing would be doing the wrong thing.
And there's a lot he could have done those first three days. He could have
called all the people together to castigate them for the sorry state of affairs.
He could have fired all the city leaders and replaced them with his own
posse. He could have assembled the people for an electrifying "I'm here to
save you" speech. He could have, but he didn't. Instead, he started his term
as governor by saying . . .

LET'S TAKE A WALK

It is not unusual when a new leader arrives to sequester him or her
in a conference room with the key senior staff and bombard the new boss
with hours of PowerPoint presentations to make sure he or she has a clear
picture of the situation—good or bad. If the situation is good, the focus
is on who gets the credit (the current management team or long-time
associate pastor or assistant principal or the engineering department or
whoever else gets to be in the meeting). If the situation is bad, the focus
can be on who (China or the worship leader) or what (the economy or
lousy products) should be blamed. The entire view of things is from the

perspective of and through the filters of the senior staff who have the most to gain and the most to lose.

That was the plan in the mid-90s when I arrived as the new leader of a West Coast aerospace machining company (unnamed to protect the innocent and the guilty). The owners had asked me to merge it with our Nashville operation because it was losing money and angering its customers with late and poor-quality parts. Machined parts for a Boeing 777 (or any other Boeing or Airbus airplane) are manufactured to tolerances within a few thousandths of an inch in high-tech, clean, organized, efficient facilities. At least they are supposed to be. After handshakes and a cup of coffee, the executive team was ready with the PowerPoint. However, I scuttled that plan with "let's take a walk first." After more than thirty years in the aerospace business, I knew I could learn a lot just by walking around.

We exited the conference room, put on safety glasses, and stepped outside. The facility looked more like the *Sanford and Son* junkyard (a 1970s hit TV comedy series starring Redd Foxx—check it out on tvland.com) than an aerospace facility. The first thing I saw was a couple of acres littered with rusting truck doors, old machines, barrels full of who-knows-what, obsolete tools, and piles of scrapped parts. Inside the buildings, the aisles were so cluttered with half-finished parts that it was hard to walk from one machine to the next. The paperwork for each job was scattered and oil-stained. I half expected Redd Foxx himself to rush up and fake a heart attack (his ploy on the TV show when things were going bad). Because of what I saw with my own eyes, I knew "the fix" would take a total change in management and months of hard work. I learned more in a thirty-minute walk-around than I would have learned in eight hours of presentations.

Now I am not suggesting that senior staff teams always deploy a smoke screen when a new leader arrives, and I am not suggesting all presentations should be cancelled. As a new leader, you need the perspective of the senior staff. However, that is not the only perspective you need. You need to hear from a lot of people, and you need to see a lot of things with your own eyes.

When Anne Mulcahy became CEO of Xerox in 2001, her first action was: "I spent the first ninety days on planes traveling to various offices and listening to anyone who had a perspective on what was wrong with the company."[52] She must have listened well because in 2008 she was named CEO of the Year by *Chief Executive* magazine. In his terrific 1989 book *Leadership*

Is an Art, Max De Pree (then CEO of the Herman Miller Company) said, "The first responsibility of a leader is to *define reality* (emphasis mine)."[53] That is what Anne Mulcahy was doing her first ninety days, and that is what Louis Gerstner Jr. was doing when IBM went "dark for a bit." And *that* is what Nehemiah was doing when he "set out during the night" to inspect the walls himself.

You may not agree with De Pree that defining reality is a leader's first responsibility, but if you have been in leadership for long, you know that it is a prime responsibility, and one you have to get right. Why is it so important? Because as a leader, you regularly make decisions—big ones—that can determine the destiny of your organization. Two of the most important ingredients in decision making are the amount and quality of the information available. When you have enough information and it is accurate, you have a great chance of making the right decision. Unfortunately, you can't always wait for that, and one of the arts and risks of leadership is making good decisions with less information than you would like to have. However, the *highest risk* is not lack of information but *wrong information.* Making decisions with wrong information can lead down a path that has a no U-turn, bridge-out crash waiting at the end. You are not leading in a parallel universe or in a virtual world. You are leading in an ever-changing "new reality." That's why I think De Pree was right: defining reality should be your first responsibility.

Elvis Presley recorded one of the most famous variations of the song "Fools Rush In." One of the lines—speaking of falling in love—claims that "wise men say only fools rush in, but I can't help falling in love with you." I have learned that "fools rush in" may be okay in love, but it better not be the normal mode of your leadership. Anne Mulcahy didn't rush in to Xerox; Louis Gerstner Jr. didn't rush in to IBM; and Nehemiah didn't rush in to Jerusalem. They all started their term as new sheriff with, "Cancel the parade. Let's take a walk. I need time to stop, look, and listen."

Leadership STONE 7   STOP, LOOK, AND LISTEN.

One of the most important lessons we learn as children is how to cross the street safely. Street crossings start in Momma's arms or in a stroller. As toddlers, we cross by holding Daddy's hand. At some point, the big day comes when we cross alone. Although I grew up in small towns with very little traffic, I'm sure I heard "stop, look, and listen" a thousand times before I ventured into the street alone. It's a formula that works for children crossing the street—and for leaders taking on a new challenge.

It worked for Nehemiah. It will work for you.

Is your organization in a mess because you rushed in to make a big splash before you knew the real situation?

How long has it been since you took a walk down the hall, looking into every corner and every closet?

Would it make any difference in your leadership if you spent ninety days listening—really listening—to the ordinary people in your organization?

When you want to "inspect the walls," do you have a few close associates with you who will tell you the truth?

What—really—is your attitude: "I'm here to save you" or "I'm here to help you"?

Are you willing to admit to a "fools rush in" start and ask your associates or congregation to let you try again? ■

8

THE NEXT BIG THING

If you don't know where you're going,
you'll end up somewhere else.[54]
YOGI BERRA

Today was amazing, a really great day. Nehemiah went public this morning on the city square. It was packed. Everyone was there: Eliashib (high priest!), the other priests, assorted officials from Jerusalem and most every surrounding village, along with hundreds of merchants, farmers, and craftsmen. They all wanted to see what Nehemiah looked like and hear what he had to say about their many concerns and questions:

Does he plan to raise taxes?

Will all the young men be drafted for some new war the king is launching?

How big a governor's palace does he want to build—and where?

How much food and wine will he confiscate to feed his family, friends, and all the official visitors who come to town?

Or is his arrival much ado about nothing—"same old, same old"?

The first big surprise came when he showed up at the square by himself. No guards. No posse. No entourage. I admit; it made me a little nervous. Instead of wearing a governor's robe, he had on working man's clothes, and for a while, he just stood there silent until the crowd quieted down. Then he stunned them by announcing he was in Jerusalem to help them do the very thing they most wanted to do: rebuild the wall! No new taxes. No new armies. No new confiscations. He didn't chew them out for the condition of the wall. He simply said, "It's down. We're in trouble. We're going to rebuild it." Everything was "we" and "us," not "you" and "me."

They were dubious at first, but his approach really got their attention. And when he shared how God had granted him favor with the king and then read aloud the king's letter, they got downright excited. He ratcheted up their hope several notches and clinched the deal when he told them he would be hauling rocks alongside them.

As what he said began to sink in, applause began to spread throughout the crowd, and soon they were shouting, "Let's get started! Let's get started!" It took Nehemiah a few minutes to quiet the crowd. Then he got down to business. He set up a meeting with all the city officials and heads of families to plan the work and asked everyone else to go home, get their tools, and show up tomorrow morning ready to start.

It's been a long time since I've seen so many smiles in Jerusalem. I can hardly wait for tomorrow.

NEHEMIAH'S JOURNAL

"The officials did not know where I had gone or what I was doing, because as yet I had said nothing to the Jews or the priests or nobles or officials or any others who would be doing the work. Then I said to them, 'You see the trouble we are in: Jerusalem lies in ruins, and its gates have been burned with fire. Come, let us rebuild the wall of Jerusalem, and we will no longer be in disgrace.' I also told them about the gracious hand of my God upon me and what the king had said to me. They replied, 'Let us start rebuilding.' So they began this good work."
(Nehemiah 2:16–18 NIV)

"THE *EAGLE* HAS LANDED"

As I write this, a crew of six International Space Station astronauts is circling the earth at just over 17,000 mph and passing about 200 miles or so above my home in Franklin, Tennessee, every 92 minutes. The space station has orbited earth more than 60,000 times in the almost eleven years it has been up there. It is so routine that weeks pass without any mention of it at all on the evening news. But it hasn't always been that way.

On October 4, 1957, the Soviet Union shocked the world by launching the first ever earth-orbiting satellite, Sputnik 1, jumping ahead of the United States in the space race. To us, it was a clash of good versus evil, God versus atheists, capitalism versus communism, and democracy versus dictatorship—and the "bad guys" were winning.

Four years later, on April 12, 1961, the Soviets were still ahead when astronaut Yuri Gagarin became the first man to orbit earth—one time around in a Vostok spacecraft. About three weeks later, the US response was feeble by comparison. It consisted of a fifteen-minute flight by astronaut Alan Shepard in which his Freedom 7 craft didn't even go into earth orbit. It would be another year before the US matched the Soviets by circling the earth (John Glenn, one time around in Friendship 7). We were behind and not catching up. Why? We were in a race, but we didn't have a finish line, a goal, a clear vision.

Vision is the responsibility of leadership, both to cast it and to pull it off. President John Kennedy was our leader in the early 1960s. It was his job to do something, and boy, did he! Six weeks after Gagarin's feat, President Kennedy cast a vision that energized America like no other in my lifetime. He shared it in a speech to a special joint session of Congress on May 25, 1961:

> I believe this nation should commit itself to achieving the goal, before this decade is out, of landing a man on the Moon and returning him safely to Earth. No single space project in this period will be more impressive to mankind, or more important in the long-range exploration of space; and none will be so difficult or expensive to accomplish.

This wasn't just an ordinary, garden-variety vision. It was a full-blown BHAG! (Big Hairy Audacious Goal, per Jim Collins in *Built to Last*.[55]) Before the US had orbited the earth even one time, President Kennedy challenged us to go to the moon and back within the next nine years! And notice he admitted that it wouldn't be easy. He said it would be "difficult . . . expensive to accomplish." He also said it would be worth it: "No single space project . . . will be more impressive . . . or more important . . . ." Two years later, President Kennedy was struck down by an assassin's bullet and didn't get to see the vision he had laid out fulfilled. But it was—and how!

On July 20, 1969, eight years and fifty-six days after President Kennedy's speech, the Apollo 11 lunar module landed on the moon, announced by astronaut Neil Armstrong's simple statement, "The *Eagle* has landed." About six hours later, at 10:56 EDT, Armstrong's left foot touched the moon's surface. Six hundred million people watched, spellbound, on live TV as the astronaut spoke his now-legendary words: "That's one small step for a man, one giant leap for mankind." Even more stirring for me was the planting of the US flag and astronaut Buzz Aldrin's pause to salute it. I am not ashamed to admit that I shed some tears that night and then again four days later when the command module *Columbia* splashed down in the Pacific Ocean, announced again with an Armstrong understatement: "Everything's okay. Our checklist is complete. Awaiting swimmers."

It had started with a surprising and shocking vision that "this nation should commit itself to achieving the goal, before this decade is out, of landing a man on the Moon and returning him safely to Earth." It wasn't a Saturn rocket that launched Apollo 11; it was a vision.

DON'T LEAVE THE TENT WITHOUT IT

In the 1970s, two television commercials promoted great themes I still remember today. One was: "American Express—don't leave home without it." The other was (I was living in Texas at the time): "If you don't have an oil well, get one. You'll love doing business with the Western Company."

Borrowing those themes and applying them to leadership yields: "Vision—don't leave your tent without it" and "Vision—if you don't have one, get one."

Why is vision so important? Significant accomplishment always requires significant vision. That is worth repeating: significant accomplishment always requires significant vision. Frankly, I can't think of *any* exceptions. In his book *Visioneering*, Andy Stanley says that it is vision that helps you "end up somewhere on purpose."[56] Bill Hybels, in *Courageous Leadership*, calls vision "A Leader's Most Potent Weapon."[57] And long before either of these men, God let us know that "where there is no vision, the people perish" (Proverbs 29:18 KJV). Recent versions of Proverbs 29:18 say that without vision, the people "run wild" (HCSB) or "are unrestrained" (NASB).

Effective leaders who accomplish big things are always guided by a compelling vision for the future. Ronald Reagan envisioned a world free from the yoke of communism. Martin Luther King Jr. envisioned a world free from prejudice. Mother Teresa envisioned a world without homeless children. And Nehemiah envisioned Jerusalem without the disgrace of fallen walls and burned gates.

Vision is crucial to significant accomplishment and enduring change because it provides two things: direction and motivation. A clear and compelling vision becomes the basis for every decision an organization makes. Vision provides the tight focus needed to develop both strategic and tactical plans. It keeps the organization from "running wild" and becoming distracted. Distractions bleed off resources—time, energy, money—to things not central to the vision. Every organization has professional rabbit chasers, but vision will keep them in their cages. Any question that comes up in the course of business should be answered based on whether it advances the vision or hinders it:

- Will this acquisition help us achieve our vision?
- Do we need a new worship center?
- Should we spend scarce R&D dollars on this project?
- Is it time to discontinue this product . . . or this ministry?

Decision making is much less blurry when there is clarity of vision to guide the process.

In addition to direction, vision is the source of motivation for significant change and accomplishment. Warren Bennis, who pioneered the study of leadership and has written more than thirty books on the subject, says that a leader "has to be able to change an organization that is dreamless, soulless and visionless. Someone's got to make a wake-up call."[58] In other words, when there is no hope, the leader's job is to fan the fire of hope for the future. How? The primary tool for hope-building is vision. A compelling vision of the future does three things: (1) it gives incentive to start, (2) it provides stamina to keep going when the road seems long, and (3) it supplies the courage to fight through tough times.

Few leaders have faced a more "dreamless, soulless and visionless" crowd than Nehemiah when he stood before the downtrodden people of Jerusalem. The walls had been down for a long time. "Walls down" was normal to them, and a previous attempt to build the walls had been stopped by the king. They had enemies on all sides who opposed rebuilding the walls. All of them already had day jobs: wheat to harvest, cloth to weave, merchandise to sell. They truly needed a wake-up call when Nehemiah stepped up to the plate that morning and declared, "You see the trouble we are in: Jerusalem lies in ruins, and its gates have been burned with fire. Come, let us rebuild the wall of Jerusalem, and we will no longer be in disgrace."

CASTING VISION

Writing about vision is difficult for me. Although I understand the critical need for vision, I am not a great visionary. My primary leadership strengths lie more in the areas of strategy and execution. However, I recognize a great vision when I see one, and Nehemiah hit a homerun with his. He touched all four bases as he stood before the people and challenged them to rebuild the walls.

First base: *We, not me*. Nehemiah's challenge was loaded with "*you . . . we . . . let us . . . we . . . .*" Nehemiah knew *his* vision had to become *their* vision. A hard truth for you as a leader to accept is that nobody cares about your vision. I'm sorry, but that's the way it is. A leader's first vision-casting objective is to transfer ownership of the vision from self to her business associates or his congregation or to whomever. The only way to do this is for the vision to be "we, not me" focused. Kouzes and Posner, in writing about vision in *The Leadership Challenge*, make it clear: "Exemplary leaders have a passion for their institution, their causes, their technologies, their communities—something other than their own fame and fortune."[59]

The divine right of kings, CEOs, and senior pastors is a dead concept even though some leaders still operate as though it is valid. Leaders should be shepherds, not dictators. Significant change and accomplishment only happen and endure when people willingly follow the leader, and that only happens with a "we, not me" vision, one that motivates people to take on a big challenge that is in their best interest, not just the leader's. I love the way Lewis Carroll put it in *Through the Looking Glass*: "He was part of my dream, of course—but then I was part of his dream, too."[60]

Second base: Clarity. Nehemiah kept it short, simple, and clear: *let us rebuild the wall of Jerusalem.* My favorite short, simple, and clear vision of all time is: "We are going to be making fewer Fiats and more Mercedes." This is an actual vision statement of a company that wanted to change its product line so it would be perceived as "different, highly recognizable . . . prestigious . . . have significantly higher prices and margins" (from John P. Kotter's superb book *Leading Change*).[61] Everyone in the company knew the difference between a Fiat and a Mercedes. Accountants as well as engineers could be guided by such a simple and clear vision. Nehemiah didn't clutter the vision with a lot of extraneous stuff. No "and then we'll . . . " or "along with . . . " or "in addition to . . . ." It was short and simple: let's rebuild the walls. Whatever would come next could wait.

Vision clutter is often the result of confusing vision with mission/purpose and trying to cast a vision that will last forever. Mission/purpose should last forever (or at least a long time), but vision doesn't. Vision is a clear picture of what the "next big thing" is. One of the best examples of unchanging mission ("turn irreligious people into fully devoted followers of Jesus Christ") and ever-changing, expanding vision is that of the Willow Creek Community Church of South Barrington, Illinois. The church was founded in 1975 by Bill Hybels, first fulfilling their mission by meeting in the Willow Creek Theatre. In 1981, the South Barrington campus opened, and then (more or less in order) came the Willow Creek Association, the Willow Creek Leadership Summit, additional campuses throughout the Chicago area, expansion of the South Barrington campus, taking the Leadership Summit worldwide, and who knows what is next. I suspect that Pastor Hybels did not cast vision for all these things back in 1975 when he launched the church. The vision and accomplishment have been progressive and changing, but the mission has been enduring and unchanging. So don't make the following mistakes:

- Don't confuse mission with vision. Mission is your reason for existing; vision is a picture of the future.
- Don't fall victim to vision clutter. Vision is a short, simple, clear picture of the next big thing. Don't clutter it with your bucket list (although it is okay to share long-term dreams with your "kitchen cabinet" or spouse).

Third base: Engage the heart. Except for engineers (I'm one) and accountants, it is emotion, not reason, that moves people to action. Nehemiah didn't appeal only to the mind, "You see the trouble we are in." He appealed to the heart, "We will no longer be in *cherpah*." (The Hebrew word *cherpah* carries the meaning of disgrace, reproach, shame, contempt, reviled, taunted, and scorned.) Here's more hard truth. Business leader, a vision for higher profits, bigger bonuses, and richer stockholders will not engage the hearts of your employees who have to rebuild the wall one stone at a time. Pastor, a vision for being the biggest church in town will not engage the hearts of your congregation. If you want to accomplish something significant, you need a significant vision that is much more than just getting bigger or richer. And by the way, don't expect to engage the hearts of your people if *your* heart isn't truly engaged. You can't fool them.

Home plate: Doable. Most people are not inclined to engage in *Mission Impossible* adventures. They may believe a vision is a great idea, but they also need to believe there is a reasonable chance of success before they will jump in with their time, energy, or money. Nehemiah had three things going for him that provided hope for success:

- His vision to rebuild the wall was based on reality. He had inspected the wall himself; he wasn't blind to the task at hand. Further, he knew—and the people knew—that the walls had stood tall and strong before.

- The resources were available to get the job done. The stones they needed were readily available as piles of rubble under the weeds, and the timbers for the gates would be supplied because "I told them . . . what the king had said to me." Two of a leader's primary responsibilities are to provide whatever is necessary to get the job done and to remove whatever obstacles stand in the way. Nehemiah did both.

- The most important thing that made rebuilding the walls doable was "I also told them about the gracious hand of my God upon me."

There is really no substitute for that. How can any of us top "What is impossible with men is possible with God" (Luke 18:27 HCSB)? Especially in the world of Christian ministry, this is where the credibility of the leader is paramount. In *The 21 Irrefutable Laws of Leadership,* John Maxwell emphasizes that "if he has not built credibility with his people, it doesn't really matter how great a vision he has."[62] It is easy to walk onto the platform and declare that God has given you a new vision for the future. It is a lot harder to build the credibility needed for your congregation to buy in wholeheartedly that it is really God's vision, not just yours.

Nehemiah hit a home run, but vision casting doesn't always go so quickly. Sometimes you get to home plate the slow way—a single, a walk, an error, a passed ball. The point is, you need buy-in, and more often than not It will take some time. Don't be discouraged if you don't score the first time you come to the plate. Buy-in is essential, so take whatever time is required to get it, and be ready to accept that it may take longer than you want it to.

Nehemiah stood before the people, cast a vision to rebuild the walls of Jerusalem, and "they replied, 'Let us start rebuilding.'" But guess what? That was the easy part.

VISION IS THE EASY PART

Every good idea—every vision—is a lot of work for someone. There are a lot more visions unfulfilled than fulfilled. Why? Poor execution.

In their best-selling 2002 book *Execution,* Larry Bossidy and Ram Charan make it painfully clear that "unless you translate big thoughts into concrete steps for action, they're pointless."[63] They also say, "Many people regard execution as detail work that's beneath the dignity of a . . . leader. That's wrong. To the contrary, it's the leader's most important job."[64] The leader's *most important* job? Yes, and Warren Bennis agrees: "Leadership is the capacity to translate vision into reality."[65]

I love these quotes because as a nonvisionary, I admit I'm more than a bit biased toward action. Without action, the "next big thing" soon becomes the "last abandoned thing." So don't fall into the trap of believing that if you are great at casting vision, you are a great leader. Great leaders may or may not be good at casting vision, but they will *always* be great at getting things done. Leaders are remembered for great accomplishments, not for great dreams.

When Nehemiah cast vision for the people of Jerusalem, not one stone had been moved. They had weeks of hard, exhausting labor in front of them. There would be frightening external opposition to overcome. Internal dissension and strife would threaten to divide the troops and stop the work. Nehemiah would face betrayal and a negative ad campaign intended to undermine his leadership. All of this would test his mettle as a leader, and failing at any point could bring the work to a screeching halt and kill the vision. So when Nehemiah cried out "Come, let us rebuild the wall of Jerusalem, and we will no longer be in disgrace" and the people responded with "Let us start rebuilding," the easy part was done. The hard part was still in front of them all.

After John Maxwell said this about leaders: "If he has not built credibility with his people, it doesn't really matter how great a vision he has,"[66] he went on to say that when a leader does have credibility, "They will follow their leader no matter how bad conditions get or how much the odds are stacked against them."[67] There is no greater example of this than Ernest Shackleton's leadership of the Imperial Trans-Antarctic Expedition in 1914–1917:

> Disaster struck this expedition when its ship, *Endurance*, became trapped in pack ice and was slowly crushed before the shore parties could be landed. There followed a sequence of exploits, and an ultimate escape with no lives lost, that would eventually assure Shackleton's heroic status.[68]

The conditions were as bad as they could get, and the odds against their survival were too high to calculate. Yet Shackleton brought the entire crew of twenty-seven safely through a twenty-month ordeal of unimaginable severity. (The full story is in *Endurance* by Caroline Alexander, a must-read for every serious student of leadership.)

It was a good thing for Nehemiah that Maxwell's credibility principle is right because before the wall was finished, conditions got bad, and the odds against them got higher. Does the leader have to cast a clear and compelling vision? Yes, without a doubt. But if the leader doesn't follow with an equally clear and compelling plan of action, the vision will not even get off the ground. It will remain nothing more than another unfulfilled dream.

Leadership STONE **8** USE THE BOX COVER.

Leading without vision is like trying to put a puzzle together without the picture on the box cover—it's almost impossible. Your vision doesn't have to be a BHAG like going to the moon. Whether it is a hundred-piece or a thousand-piece puzzle, it has to give you and your followers something clear and compelling to shoot at and to guide your strategy and tactics. Vision is the leader's picture of the next big thing. If it is fuzzy to you, it will be more so to your organization. So keep the box cover on the table to continually remind everyone of what you are trying to accomplish.

Is your organization floundering, frustrated, getting tired, and going nowhere? Maybe you are running a race without aim, without a finish line, without a vision.

Are you the leader? It's up to you. Get out your paintbrush and start painting a picture of the future. Your business or church or nonprofit or family or _____ is waiting for you.

If you have already cast vision and it didn't take hold, is it a "we not me" vision?

Does it have clarity, or is it fuzzy or cluttered?

Does the *next big thing* you want to do engage the heart of your employees, congregation, or volunteers? Does it engage *your* heart?

Is it doable, or do your followers think it's a pipe dream?

If your vision is clear but going nowhere, then either you as the leader or the "get-it-done" plan are lacking credibility. Do you know which it is? Go to work on whichever one it is. ■

9

A HARD HAT FOR EVERYONE

Good leaders make people feel that they're at the very heart of things,
not at the periphery. Everyone feels that he or she
makes a difference to the success of the organization.[69]

WARREN BENNIS

What an unforgettable day. The sky was light, but the sun wasn't up yet when Nehemiah rousted me out of bed with a loud, "Get your work clothes on!" After I dressed, we headed for the wall, or rather, the pile of rubble that would become a wall. Much to my surprise, we weren't the first ones there. Several hundred people were already at work clearing away 142 years' worth of weeds and debris. They were burning big piles of brush, and we could already see some stones uncovered from the original wall. And a steady stream of people was still arriving. They were coming from all the districts of Jerusalem and even from places like Jericho and Keilah—ten or more miles away!

Eliashib's crew was clearing away debris near the Sheep Gate. A lot of merchants had closed their shops for the day, and even the goldsmiths and perfumers were getting their hands dirty. I bet they have never had calluses before. Some of the women were bringing water to the workers, and a few were actually working alongside the men, doing as much of the heavy lifting as they could.

The early arrivers were so into their work that some of those who came later ended up just milling around, not sure where to start or what to do. As soon as Nehemiah realized what was happening, he (of course) took charge to get things organized. He called all the leaders and chiefs together, asked for their input, decided who would do what, and then sent them out to make assignments. For sure, the plan will have to be tweaked as we go along, but by the end of the day, it looked like everybody knew what they were doing.

After his morning of organizing the supervisors, Nehemiah spent the rest of the day walking around the wall, encouraging people and thanking them for coming. He was also very good about asking them what they need for the job. At the end of the day, he scheduled a meeting of all the leaders for 7:00 a.m. tomorrow to review progress, discuss problems, and make any changes needed in work assignments.

Right now, the sun is slipping below the horizon, and there are campfires all over the hillsides as people prepare their evening meals. They'll sleep well tonight. I think most everyone is pretty excited about what happened today. Nehemiah wandered off by himself a few minutes ago, probably for evening prayers. I'm headed for bed. This has been awesome, but I'm worn out. If we can manage to keep up the pace, we just may pull this off.

NEHEMIAH'S JOURNAL

"Eliashib the high priest and his fellow priests went to work and rebuilt the Sheep Gate. They dedicated it and set its doors in place, building as far as the Tower of the Hundred, which they dedicated, and as far as the Tower of Hananel.

"The men of Jericho built the adjoining section, and Zaccur son of Imri built next to them. The Fish Gate was rebuilt by the sons of Hassenaah. They laid its beams and put its doors and bolts and bars in place.

"Meremoth son of Uriah, the son of Hakkoz, repaired the next section. Next to him Meshullam son of Berekiah, the son of Meshezabel, made repairs, and next to him Zadok son of Baana also made repairs. The next section was repaired by the men of Tekoa, but their nobles would not put their shoulders to the work under their supervisors.

"The Jeshanah Gate was repaired by Joiada son of Paseah and Meshullam son of Besodeiah. They laid its beams and put its doors and bolts and bars in place.

Next to them, repairs were made by men from Gibeon and Mizpah—Melatiah of Gibeon and Jadon of Meronoth—places under the authority of the governor of Trans-Euphrates.

"Uzziel son of Harhaiah, one of the goldsmiths, repaired the next section; and Hananiah, one of the perfume-makers, made repairs next to that. They restored Jerusalem as far as the Broad Wall.

"Rephaiah son of Hur, ruler of a half-district of Jerusalem, repaired the next section. Adjoining this, Jedaiah son of Harumaph made repairs opposite his house, and Hattush son of Hashabneiah made repairs next to him. Malkijah son of Harim and Hasshub son of Pahath-Moab repaired another section and the Tower of the Ovens.

"Shallum son of Hallohesh, ruler of a half-district of Jerusalem, repaired the next section with the help of his daughters. The Valley Gate was repaired by Hanun and the residents of Zanoah. They rebuilt it and put its doors and bolts and bars in place. They also repaired five hundred yards of the wall as far as the Dung Gate. The Dung Gate was repaired by Malkijah son of Recab, ruler of the district of Beth Hakkerem. He rebuilt it and put its doors and bolts and bars in place.

"The Fountain Gate was repaired by Shallun son of Col-Hozeh, ruler of the district of Mizpah. He rebuilt it, roofing it over and putting its doors and bolts and bars in place. He also repaired the wall of the Pool of Siloam, by the King's Garden, as far as the steps going down from the City of David.

"Beyond him, Nehemiah son of Azbuk, ruler of a half-district of Beth Zur, made repairs up to a point opposite the tombs of David, as far as the artificial pool and the House of the Heroes. Next to him, the repairs were made by the Levites under Rehum son of Bani. Beside him, Hashabiah, ruler of half the district of Keilah, carried out repairs for his district. Next to him, the repairs were made by their countrymen under Binnui son of Henadad, ruler of the other half-district of Keilah. Next to him, Ezer son of Jeshua, ruler of Mizpah, repaired another section, from a point facing the ascent to the armory as far as the angle. Next to him, Baruch son of Zabbai zealously repaired another section, from the angle to the entrance of the house of Eliashib the high priest.

Next to him, Meremoth son of Uriah, the son of Hakkoz, repaired another section, from the entrance of Eliashib's house to the end of it. The repairs next to him were made by the priests from the surrounding region.

"Beyond them, Benjamin and Hasshub made repairs in front of their house; and next to them, Azariah son of Maaseiah, the son of Ananiah, made repairs beside his house. Next to him, Binnui son of Henadad repaired another section, from Azariah's house to the angle and the corner, and Palal son of Uzai worked opposite the angle and the tower projecting from the upper palace near the court of the guard. Next to him, Pedaiah son of Parosh and the temple servants living on the hill of Ophel made repairs up to a point opposite the Water Gate toward the east and the projecting tower. Next to them, the men of Tekoa repaired another section, from the great projecting tower to the wall of Ophel.

"Above the Horse Gate, the priests made repairs, each in front of his own house. Next to them, Zadok son of Immer made repairs opposite his house. Next to him, Shemaiah son of Shecaniah, the guard at the East Gate, made repairs. Next to him, Hananiah son of Shelemiah, and Hanun, the sixth son of Zalaph, repaired another section. Next to them, Meshullam son of Berekiah made repairs opposite his living quarters. Next to him, Malkijah, one of the goldsmiths, made repairs as far as the house of the temple servants and the merchants, opposite the Inspection Gate, and as far as the room above the corner; and between the room above the corner and the Sheep Gate the goldsmiths and merchants made repairs." (Nehemiah 3:1–32 NIV)

NO EXPERIENCE REQUIRED

It is common today for women to work in heavy industry factories. They do all the things men do on assembly lines, in machine shops, in quality labs, and stockrooms. But that hasn't always been the case. It started during World War II when the men were off fighting, and workers were needed to produce airplanes, tanks, rifles, jeeps, and bullets. Women stepped up and were immortalized in a hit song, "Rosie the Riveter":

All the day long, whether rain or shine,
She's part of the assembly line.
She's making history, working for victory,
Rosie the Riveter[70]

It's not an exaggeration to say that without thousands of Rosies, the war would have dragged on for years longer than it did. The women had no experience, but they were motivated to get the job done—and they did.

I had my own Rosie the Riveter experience in the late '80s. While serving as VP of Finance for a midsize aerospace company, we were confronted with a crippling thirteen-week strike. At least it could have been crippling, but it wasn't. Why? Because accountants, secretaries, engineers, buyers, vice-presidents, and even the lawyers all "went to the factory floor" to keep production going. Since they didn't trust me with anything that moved or made noise, I was a wing wiper, meaning I took a rag, squirted Trike (trichloroethylene) on it, and cleaned excess adhesive, oil, dirt, and grime off of aluminum surfaces before they went to the paint shop. We were organized, inspired, and well led by our president, John Kleban. For thirteen weeks, our motley crew, by working hard with enthusiasm, kept the production lines moving and our customers satisfied. That is when the value of a hard hat for everyone was indelibly imprinted into my leadership DNA. Nehemiah knew about that a long time before I did.

In today's world, a wall-building project takes months of planning and engineering, more months of seeking building permits, followed by even more months of evaluating bids and choosing a contractor. Finally, the work begins. But Nehemiah didn't have to go through all that. He couldn't call on Precision Wall Building, Inc., or the Wall Building Specialists of Jerusalem to do the work. Nehemiah 2:19 (NIV) says, "They put their hands to the good work." So who were *they*? Everyone! The priests, the leaders of families and districts, farmers, shopkeepers, and Nehemiah himself. They all got their hands dirty. The Israelite Rosies worked alongside the men, and you didn't have to be a construction worker to get on the job. Goldsmiths and perfumers did their share, too. There were no benchwarmers on Nehemiah's team. He found a spot for everyone—and as we'll see, the right spot.

Nehemiah had a huge task in front of him. There were 7,500 feet of walls to rebuild, plus ten gates and five towers to repair. A good start was imperative—it always is. Nothing will kill a project faster than stumbling on the front end. Early success is crucial to long-term success. So Nehemiah started by using three important "i" tenets: he *inspired* the people with vision, he *included* everyone, and he was *intentional* with the work assignments. And those three "i's" still work today. Are they in your leadership toolbox?

"PLAN" IS *NOT* A FOUR-LETTER WORD

In the last fifteen to twenty years, there has been a school of thought that leaders are above the nitty gritty. Their job is to cast vision, inspire the minions, and then leave the planning and execution to managers who are good at details but "not quite up to leading." Most of the words that come to my mind about this reasoning are not appropriate for this book. The very reason that Larry Bossidy and Ram Charan wrote *Execution* was to debunk this idea. In chapter 8, I included a quote which summarizes the main point of their book: "Unless you translate big thoughts into concrete steps for action, they're pointless."[71]

Let me be clear: leaders are responsible for both vision and execution, and execution begins with "concrete steps for action"—a plan! "Plan" is not the nasty four-letter word that contemporary leadership literature often makes it out to be. My all-time favorite football coach, Tom Landry, said this: "Setting a goal is not the main thing. It is deciding how you will go about achieving it and staying with that plan."[72] Yet more important than what Tom Landry says is what God says: "The plans of the diligent lead surely to advantage" (Proverbs 21:5 NASB). In *The Message*, Eugene Peterson paraphrases the same verse this way: "Careful planning puts you ahead in the long run."

A mark of really good writing is steering clear of common and overused clichés. However, the reason some clichés are overused is because they are so true, and one is: "Failing to plan is planning to fail." If you are a leader, *planning is part of your job.* You can delegate the *task* of planning, but you cannot delegate the *responsibility* for planning. It is the leader's job to make sure it is done and done well. You cannot delegate the follow-up either. Leaders who distance themselves from planning and follow-up are sending two messages to their team: (1) this project is not important enough for me to spend time on it, and (2) if the project fails, it is your fault, not mine. Be assured, if the leader washes his hands of the project, so will the rest of the organization. Junkyards are full of projects that got there because the leader did not stay involved from beginning to end. Maybe that is why Solomon included the word *diligent* in Proverbs 21:5.

There is no way to read Nehemiah 3 without concluding that the wall-building project was well planned and organized. We aren't told anything about the planning process—how long it took, who was involved, and so on—but there are three things that we know for sure: the plan was detailed, it was personal, and there were no gaps. Assignments were made for every foot of the wall, for every gate and every tower, and the assignments made sense. The workers didn't need to ask, "Why am I working on the east wall?" or "Why can't I work closer to home?"

Bite-sized pieces. I don't know if Henry Ford ever read chapter 3 of Nehemiah, but if he did, he would have given Nehemiah high marks for planning and organization. Ford—who revolutionized assembly-line manufacturing—once said, "Nothing is particularly hard if you divide it into small jobs."[73] That is exactly what Nehemiah and his planning team did. They divided the project into bite-sized jobs so that no group felt overwhelmed by the task.

Rebuilding 1½ miles of wall, along with its gates and towers, is a huge task without bulldozers, cranes, and cement trucks—but not overwhelming. Why? Because Nehemiah and his planning team divided the task among thirty-seven different work groups. Most worked on the wall, but a few focused only on the gates or towers. Because some groups had the ability to do more (details later), the assignment for most groups was only about 50 yards of wall to a height of about 20 feet. So when the men from Gibeon and Mizpah arrived at the construction site for the first time, they probably heard something like this from their leaders, Melatiah and Jadon:

> Our job is to rebuild the part of the wall from the Old Gate to a point fifty yards to the south, where Uzziel's team will take over. Working five days a week, if we raise the wall about six inches per day, we can finish in less than two months. We'll have a couple of days each week to take care of things back home, and by working hard and working together, we can do it. Everyone is counting on us to do our part, so let's get started.

I confess that I don't know for sure that the Melatiah and Jadon team assignment was only 50 yards. The point is, there is a world of difference between looking at the project as a 1½ mile, 20-foot-high burden versus a 50 yard, 6-inches-a-day task.

At one point in my aerospace career, our company manufactured a product that needed a 50 percent reduction in cost if we were to be competitive and keep the work from going overseas. The near-unanimous reaction of manufacturing, procurement, and engineering was, "No way. That's impossible." But when we reframed the challenge as reducing cost by 5 percent, then doing it again, and again, and . . . , the reaction was a positive, "Let's go for it." The 50 percent goal was monstrous, but the plan to get there in a series of bite-size steps made it doable. That was Nehemiah's strategy, and it's still a good one.

Personal. A second feature that made Nehemiah's plan effective was that it was personal. Few things will cause a project to stumble or bog down more than "This plan doesn't make sense to me." Nehemiah 3 is full of phrases like "in front of his house . . . opposite his house . . . beside his house." I suppose there were a lot of places Jedaiah could have worked, but what was most personal and made the most sense was "Jedaiah made repairs opposite his house" (Nehemiah 3:10 NIV). Imagine his enthusiasm when he told his wife that he would be repairing the wall opposite their home. There was a common-sense element to this assignment (less commuting time), but the most important hook was emotional. It always is. Things that engage people's hearts are much better motivators than things that only engage their minds.

No gaps. Nehemiah 3:2 (NIV) says, "The men of Jericho built the adjoining section, and Zakkur son of Imri built *next to* them" (emphasis mine). The words "next to" are used twenty-eight times in Nehemiah 3. The point? There were no gaps in the plan. Every foot of the wall, every gate, and every tower were assigned to someone. One of the reasons for planning is to make sure nothing important is missed. Even though Nehemiah's journal doesn't explain the process used to develop the plan, I'm pretty sure of this: Nehemiah didn't do it by himself. In *First, Break All the Rules*, Buckingham and Coffman make this critical observation: "The most efficient route . . . is rarely a straight line. It is always the path of least resistance."[74]

If you want to ensure you have resistance to a plan, then develop it yourself and pass it down with instructions to "do this." I doubt if that worked in Nehemiah's day; I know it doesn't work today. The path of least resistance is the path developed by the people who are going to do the work. The best plans always include a lot of input from the team for two reasons: (1) you aren't smart enough to think of everything, and (2) you want the team to take ownership of the plan. "Their plan" has a much better chance of success than "your plan." Every time.

THE WALL OF FAME

Lots of organizations have them—a wall of fame, or honor—but the closest I've ever come to having my name enshrined anywhere is on the gym floor of my high school. Our basketball coach decided it was time to refinish the floor, and to save money, he had the team do the labor. We sanded the floor, stained it, and then put on two coats of polyurethane. It looked great and sounded great, squeaking when we walked on it. In one corner, on top of the stain and under the polyurethane, we wrote our names with a marker: "Major Morgan, Harold Hunter, Ray Brooks, Dick Wells." We wanted to make sure everyone would know who refinished the floor. That gym was long ago replaced by a new one, so the floor of fame with my name on it had a short life.

A true wall of fame displays a long-term reminder of the names, and often pictures, of exceptional performers or leaders. At the Congressional Medal of Honor Memorial in Indianapolis, Indiana, the names of more than 3400 recipients of the medal are etched in glass. The NFL Hall of Fame has more than 250 inductees (my favorite: Roger Staubach); the baseball Hall of Fame has about 300 (my favorite: Mickey Mantle, with Hank Aaron a close second). The Smithsonian in Washington, DC, features the Hall of Presidents (my favorites: Abraham Lincoln and Harry Truman), and most states have similar galleries to honor past governors. Hundreds of businesses, universities, and churches have memorials to their distinguished leaders. A small church in southwest Oklahoma has its own honor wall with pictures of all the pastors in its one-hundred-plus year history. I'm proud that my dad's picture is there.

Nehemiah 3 is the Wall of Fame for the wall-building project. When I read it, I visualize walking along the wall and seeing where the workers carved their names into the stones at the places where they worked: "This section rebuilt by _____"; "This section raised by _____"; "This tower repaired by _____." Starting with "Eliashib the high priest and his fellow priests" and finishing with "the goldsmiths and merchants," more than fifty individuals and groups would have had their names scratched into the stones. Imagine how proud the grandchildren of Uzziel the gold-smith and Hananiah the perfume maker would have been when they saw their grandfathers' names. I can hear them now: "There's Papa's name!"

Theodore Roosevelt once said, "The one thing I want to leave my children is an honorable name."[75] Nehemiah made sure that those who worked on the wall would be honored and remembered. How was he able to do that? He knew them and took the time to record all their names so we could know them, too.

As a leader, one of the best ways you can honor and show respect for your followers is to know them by name. It ranks right up there with lis-tening. Want to make the janitor's day? Walk up and say, "How are you doing, Jim? Thanks for keeping this place so clean." I guarantee you that Jim will tell his wife, and your workspace will be even cleaner tomorrow. I know that an organization can become so large that it is impossible to know everyone. I've been there. I once had 3,000 people working for me. I couldn't know all their names, but I made an effort to know as many as I could. It was worth it for me, and it will be for you. There are few things you can do that will raise your leadership credibility more than knowing the names of those you are trying to influence and lead.

Now . . . back to my virtual walk around the wall. About halfway around, I pause when I spot the name Meremoth. It looks familiar. Have I seen it before? Yes, on the north side near the Fish Gate. Meremoth worked on two sections of the wall. As I continue on, I see the names of Meshullam, Binnui, and the men of Tekoa for a second time. All of these finished their first assignment and asked for more. They were the "over and above, bring it on" crowd that every organization needs—the "I'll stay late" or work on Saturday champions who are often the difference between success and failure.

Continuing my walk, about halfway down the west side I see that Hanun and the inhabitants of Zanoah repaired the Valley Gate. I keep walking . . . and walking . . . and walking for more than a quarter of a mile before I see more names, and surprisingly, Hanun and the inhabit-ants of Zanoah are scratched into the wall again. Surely not. They didn't rebuild the Valley Gate and this long section of wall, did they? Referring to my Walking Tour of Nehemiah's Wall brochure ($5 at a kiosk near the Fish Gate), I am stunned to read:

Hanun and the inhabitants of Zanoah repaired the Valley Gate. They
rebuilt it and installed its doors, bolts, and bars, and repaired 500
yards of the wall to the Dung Gate. (Nehemiah 3:13 HCSB)

Wow! Don't miss this. The average group repaired about 50 yards
of the wall. A few did 100 yards. But Hanun and the inhabitants of
Zanoah did ten times the average—500 yards! They were the superstars
of the project!

Here is a truth from the athletic world that is likewise true in all kinds
of organizations: You can have a winning team with some hard-working
"over and above" players, but championship teams always have a few superstars. Exceptional accomplishment always requires exceptional performance
led by exceptional leaders. Nehemiah's exceptional accomplishment was
not just finishing the wall; it was finishing it in only fifty-two days while
facing formidable challenges and enemies. How did they do it? One group
(out of thirty-seven) did 20 percent of the work! Without Hanun and the
inhabitants of Zanoah, the wall would have been finished, but who knows
how long it would have taken.

Nehemiah deftly led all kinds of people on the project. Some weren't
able to do a lot, but they were able to do something. Others could stand
out, doing more than their share. A few were superstars. They carried the
heaviest load, far surpassing the contributions of others. It is always this way
in organizations. One of the challenges of leadership is to recognize what
people can do, turn them loose to do it, and then recognize their contri-
bution no matter how small—or large. Easy to do? No. Especially when it
comes to the matter of recognition.

Chapter 3 of Nehemiah's journal is a great example of appropriate and
effective recognition:

- Nehemiah recognized everyone by name. This is a powerful
  leadership tool.
- He was specific about what they had done—*Zadok son of
  Immer made repairs opposite his house.* He didn't use adjectives;
  he used facts.
- He did not use labels. Everyone knew who the superstars were
  without Nehemiah anointing them as such.

Recognition can be a tricky thing. However, don't shy away from
it for fear of making a mistake or leaving someone out. If you aren't sure

what to do, follow Nehemiah's example. Remember that the primary reason for recognition is to show appreciation, not create distinctions.

Leadership STONE **9** A JOB FOR EVERYONE, A PLAN FOR EVERYONE, RECOGNITION FOR EVERYONE

When it comes to execution, Leadership Stone #9 is so central to success that this chapter's opening quote by Warren Bennis is worth repeating:

Good leaders make people feel that they're at the very heart of things, not at the periphery. Everyone feels that he or she makes a difference to the success of the organization.

The key word in this quote is "everyone" and it actually does mean *everyone*—no one excluded. However, just gathering the troops to fire them up with a great speech ending with "Charge!" won't get the job done. The "makes a difference to the success" part of the quote comes from having a plan for everyone that is personal, bite-sized, and has no gaps. The larger and more complex the project, the more important the plan is. If you shortcut the planning process, some*one* will be left out and some*thing* will be left out—and your wall will have gaps.

One of the challenges of leadership is to create an environment in which both the mere mortals as well as the superstars are appreciated and can flourish. Most teams—athletic, business, ministry, and wall construction—have this mix of talent. Nehemiah had a team of mortals (they could rebuild about 50 yards), stars (they could do two sections of the wall), and superstars (they repaired a gate and then rebuilt 500 yards of wall). Nehemiah doesn't tell us why Hanun and the inhabitants of Zanoah could do so much more than everyone else or why Malkijah could repair only one gate (the Dung Gate). He simply matched their assignments to their abilities, turned them loose to do the job, and in the end, they all got their name on the Wall of Fame.

Do you have a major project that is struggling and may not make it?

Is everyone in the organization included?

Do you have a team, or just a collection of people?

Is there a specific, personal, bite-sized plan for everyone?

Is everyone being recognized and honored, or just the superstars? ■

10

NOT FOR THE THIN-SKINNED

Criticism is as inevitable as breathing.[76]

T. S. ELIOT

We've gotten a lot done in the last few weeks, but it's been tough. Building a wall is hard work anytime, but this is the hottest time of the year. We're tired and dirty at the end of every day . . . I mean . . . exhausted! When I go to bed, I'm asleep the instant I lie down. And the sun keeps coming up way too early.

At this point, Nehemiah has had to spend most of his time just encouraging the workers. Critics have come out of the woodwork, trying to halt the project. Sanballat and his cohorts aren't happy about Jerusalem becoming a walled city again. I suppose they think they will have less power and influence in the region. They make fun of the workers. Yesterday, that jerk Tobiah shouted at some of our people that the wall would collapse if a fox climbed on it.

Sanballat and his monkeys have stooped to name-calling and have started accusing us of "rebelling against the king." I guess they haven't seen the letter from King Artaxerxes authorizing the work, but that still makes me nervous. I wonder if they really could cause trouble for us with the king.

Nehemiah, though, seems unflappable. Except for an angry prayer or two, he has ignored all the critics and kept us on task. He simply tells our folks, "Don't worry about them; just keep working."

Most people have kept hard at it, so in spite of the mockers, today was a milestone—the wall is about half finished! There were a lot of smiles as people headed home this evening, seeing how much progress we've made. Of course, the higher it goes, the harder it gets.

NEHEMIAH'S JOURNAL

"When Sanballat the Horonite and Tobiah the Ammonite official heard about this, they were very much disturbed that someone had come to promote the welfare of the Israelites." (Nehemiah 2:10 NIV)

"But when Sanballat the Horonite, Tobiah the Ammonite official and Geshem the Arab heard about it, they mocked and ridiculed us. 'What is this you are doing?' they asked. 'Are you rebelling against the king?'" (Nehemiah 2:19 NIV)

"When Sanballat heard that we were rebuilding the wall, he became angry and was greatly incensed. He ridiculed the Jews, and in the presence of his associates and the army of Samaria, he said, 'What are those feeble Jews doing? Will they restore their wall? Will they offer sacrifices? Will they finish in a day? Can they bring the stones back to life from those heaps of rubble—burned as they are?' Tobiah the Ammonite, who was at his side, said, 'What they are building—if even a fox climbed up on it, he would break down their wall of stones!'" (Nehemiah 4:1-3 NIV)

THE KITCHEN IS ALWAYS HOT

About one hundred years after Nehemiah rebuilt Jerusalem's wall, the Greek philosopher Aristotle said, "Criticism is something we can avoid easily by . . . doing nothing."[77] More than 2,000 years later, President Teddy Roosevelt managed to take criticism in stride as he noted: "It behooves every man to remember that the work of the critic is of altogether secondary importance, and that, in the end, progress is accomplished by the man who does things."[78] Roosevelt's best-known assessment of criticism is:

It is not the critic who counts; not the man who points out how the strong man stumbles, or where the doer of deeds could have done them better. The credit belongs to the man who is actually in the arena, whose face is marred by dust and sweat and blood, who strives valiantly; who errs and comes short again and again; because there is not effort without error and shortcomings; but who does actually strive to do the deed; who knows the great enthusiasm, the great devotion, who spends himself in a worthy cause, who at the best knows in the end the triumph of high achievement and who at the worst, if he fails, at least he fails while daring greatly.[79]

If you want to avoid critics, then do nothing—and accomplish nothing. Don't run for president. Don't aspire to lead your company. Don't make suggestions. Don't volunteer. Don't become a pastor or school principal. Don't get "in the arena," and stay out of the kitchen. The kitchen is always hot for leaders. Leadership is not for the *thin-skinned* who wither every time the critics show up. They will always show up if you are trying to do something significant like rebuild a wall . . . or a business . . . or a church. So let me make it simple for you: if you can't handle criticism, you won't be able to lead. Nehemiah was no exception.

Like King David before him . . .

I mourned and fasted, but it brought me insults. I wore sackcloth as my clothing, and I was a joke to them. Those who sit at the city gate talk about me, and drunkards make up songs about me. (Psalm 69:10–12 HCSB)

and Jesus after him . . .

Look, a glutton and a drunkard, a friend of tax collectors and sinners! (Luke 7:34 HCSB)

Nehemiah had to cope with criticism, and so will you. How well you cope can be the difference between your success or failure as a leader. Since every leadership situation is different, there is not a one-size-fits-all formula for coping. However, fully and truthfully answering the questions below will help you respond appropriately.

Question #1—Who or what is the target? Sanballat, Tobiah, and Geshem used the shotgun approach in their first blast of criticism. Nehemiah wasn't personally named; the Jews were mocked and ridiculed as a group. They were called "feeble," their will to finish was questioned, and the quality of their work was ridiculed: "if even a fox climbed up on it, he would break down their wall of stones!" They knew they couldn't break Nehemiah's resolve to finish, so they tried to break down everyone else.

Criticism can be specific to the leader: "She's a lousy manager" or "He can't preach worth a flip." It can be directed at a group: "The factory workers are lazy" or "Management is overpaid." A project can be the target of criticism: "Buying that machine is a waste of money" or "Why on earth do we need a new building for the children's ministry?" Even though all criticism may feel personal, it isn't always personal. Recognizing the target is an important first step in deciding whether to respond and how.

Question #2—Who is the source? How often have you heard someone say, "Consider the source"? That is wise counsel. Is the critic an insider or outsider? Is the critic an enemy who would oppose most anything you try to do, or someone who usually—but not this time—supports what you try to do? Is the criticism from one person or many? Is the critic someone who believes he or she has the "gift of criticism" and feels entitled—even obligated—to exercise the gift every chance he or she gets? For Nehemiah, the answer was easy. The critics were outsiders and enemies who were *angry* and *greatly incensed*. For you, the answer may not be as clear cut, but "getting it right" is crucial to understanding the motive for the criticism, which is the next question.

Question #3—What is the motive of the criticism? Sanballat was the governor of Samaria (north of Jerusalem) and ring leader of the critics. Tobiah was governor of Ammon (east of Jerusalem), and Geshem the Arab was a ruler of the desert tribes south of Jerusalem. All three were avowed enemies of the Jews and knew their political and economic power would be diminished by the resurgence of the Jews in Judah. Their motive was clear and simple: to protect their own interests by permanently stopping reconstruction of the wall. They used ridicule and mocking to destroy the confidence and will of the people. They tried to instill fear by accusing them of *rebelling against the king*. It was obvious what Sanballat was trying to do. Again, it may not be as clear and simple for you, especially if the criticism is from internal sources instead of external enemies.

Criticism can arise internally from damaged self-interests, wounded egos, jealousy, and hurt feelings. It can be a huge distraction, sapping energy that should be focused on the task at hand. Sometimes, however, it arises internally from well-intentioned and honest disagreement. That is when honestly answering question #4 will be one of your biggest challenges.

Question #4—How true is the criticism? It is *not* true that there is a grain of truth in all criticism. There was no truth in the criticism launched at Nehemiah and his team. However, it is a serious mistake for a leader to automatically discount all criticism as untrue and irrelevant, no matter the source. Good people with good intentions are sometimes correctly criticized by good people with good intentions. That is when, like sharp sticks and jagged stones, words do actually hurt—sometimes a lot.

When criticism is directed at you, don't become defensive and assume that the intent is to hurt you. In fact, do the opposite. Presume the critic has good intent so you will search the criticism for truth with an open mind. Pay careful attention to the words used and the tone. If you aren't sure what the critic means, ask for clarification. Whether the criticism is personal or aimed at a project or group, don't try to assess the truth of it by yourself. Especially if the criticism is personal, being honestly objective about it lies somewhere between difficult and impossible. Ask people you trust, "What does this mean, and is it true?" To the extent that the criticism is true, you need to accept it no matter how painful it may be. When I was told that they hate me (see the introduction) because I was a controlling, know-it-all boss, it hurt. However, it was true, and I had to accept it. Actually, I didn't *have* to accept it, but if I hadn't, the trajectory of my career would have changed from rising to falling.

Question #5—What is the appropriate response to criticism? Whatever the target, the source, the motive, and the truth, it is the leader's responsibility to respond. Your response will flow out of the answers to the first four questions, and how a leader responds is often more important than the criticism itself. Nehemiah's response was twofold: first, he prayed; second, he ignored the critics and kept working. Nehemiah's prayer sounded a lot like one of David's in the Psalms:

> Hear us, O our God, for we are despised. Turn their insults back on their own heads. Give them over as plunder in a land of captivity. Do not cover up their guilt or blot out their sins from your sight, for they have thrown insults in the face of the builders. (Nehemiah 4:4–5 NIV)

Whether this prayer would pass muster with Jesus' "love your enemies" command, I'm not sure. I'll let you have a good discussion about that with your pastor over a cup of coffee. The important point of this prayer is not the specific words he used, but the simple fact that when faced with critics and opposition, he turned first to God for help. Instead of name-calling and trading insults with Sanballat, he said, "God, You handle it." Isn't that what Romans 12:19—"never take your own revenge"—tells us to do? After praying, Nehemiah headed back to the wall: "So we rebuilt the wall till all of it reached half its height, for the people worked with all their heart" (Nehemiah 4:6 NIV).

Your response after prayer may or may not be the same as Nehemiah's. You may—often wisely—choose to ignore the criticism and keep working, or it may be appropriate to respond to the critics. If you choose to respond, don't react quickly or in anger. Follow the guidance in these two proverbs:

> Do you see a man who speaks too soon? There is more hope for a fool than for him. (Proverbs 29:20 HCSB)

> He who is slow to anger has great understanding. (Proverbs 14:29 NASB95)

Laurence J. Peter, author of *The Peter Principle*, said it this way: "Speak when you are angry, and you'll make the best speech you'll ever regret."[80] So go slowly, be calm, and remember:

- The target of your response should be the criticism, not the critic.
- The purpose of your response should be to elevate truth, not self.
- The tone of your response should be to build up, not tear down.

And whatever you do, don't let criticism turn you into a critic.

Leadership STONE 10 LISTENING EARS, A TOUGH HIDE

As children, we all heard that "sticks and stones may break my bones, but words will never hurt me." It didn't take us long to discover it wasn't true. Words can hurt—a lot. That doesn't change when we become adults. Words still hurt, and in leadership, not only do they hurt, they are incessant. If you are easily wounded, crippled, or distracted by criticism, even when it is untrue and unfair, leadership is going to be hard for you. Effective leaders know when to ignore criticism and when and how to respond. They check their emotions at the door, and then they respond if necessary.

If you are "in the arena," criticism is certain. Are you letting it distract you and slow the momentum of your organization?

Before taking it personally, have you taken time to correctly identify the target of the criticism?

Considering the source of the criticism, is it worth considering at all?

Is it from external or internal sources?

What is the motive of the critics? Is it possible they are well-intentioned?

Rather than reject it out of hand, have you honestly examined whether it could be true or not?

If you decide you need to respond, why?

Will a response accomplish anything positive, or just inflame the critics?

Few people in our country's history were criticized more than Abraham Lincoln. His response?

Having chosen our course, without guile and with pure purpose, let us renew our trust in God, and go forward without fear and with manly hearts.[81]

That is what great leaders do when criticized. They aren't distracted. They examine themselves to make sure their motives are *without guile* and have a *pure purpose.* They pray and trust. Then they *go forward* to finish the wall. If Lincoln could handle a civil war that way, you can handle whatever comes your way . . . even words that hurt. ∎

DEFCON 1
IMMINENT ATTACK

We've had men in those silos since before any of
you guys were watching "Howdy Doody"!
Now I myself sleep pretty well knowing those boys are down there.[82]
GENERAL BERINGER IN *WAR GAMES*

The game has changed. The routine and tedious days of get up, eat breakfast, work on the wall all day, and then collapse into bed are over. Sanballat raised the stakes. Now he's threatened to attack and kill us if we don't stop working on the wall. We're on "Red Alert." As if hauling rocks isn't enough, now we have to carry weapons with us all the time, post guards 24/7, and sleep inside the half-finished walls. We're scrambling to get all the gaps closed and the low points raised as soon as possible. It has really slowed progress on the wall, but most people have stuck with us.

Nehemiah really stepped up to the plate when the first threats came in. Everyone was watching to see what he would do. As always, the first thing he did was pray, but then he was everywhere, encouraging workers, organizing defense teams, issuing weapons. On top of that, to set an example of courage, he stayed on top of the wall, visible to everyone—including Sanballat's archers!

A lot of us tried to get him to be more careful, but he ignored us. The people took courage from him, and although we're all still a little afraid, we're ready to fight if we have to. Sanballat won't surprise us now, so maybe they'll give up the idea of attacking and go home. In another month or so, the walls will be up and the gates in place. Once that's done, Sanballat can "bring it on" for all I care.

NEHEMIAH'S JOURNAL

"But when Sanballat, Tobiah, the Arabs, the Ammonites and the men of Ashdod heard that the repairs to Jerusalem's walls had gone ahead and that the gaps were being closed, they were very angry. They all plotted together to come and fight against Jerusalem and stir up trouble against it. But we prayed to our God and posted a guard day and night to meet this threat . . . . Also our enemies said, 'Before they know it or see us, we will be right there among them and will kill them and put an end to the work.' Then the Jews who lived near them came and told us ten times over, 'Wherever you turn, they will attack us.' Therefore I stationed some of the people behind the lowest points of the wall at the exposed places, posting them by families, with their swords, spears and bows." (Nehemiah 4:6–13 NIV)

"From that day on, half of my men did the work, while the other half were equipped with spears, shields, bows and armor. The officers posted themselves behind all the people of Judah who were building the wall. Those who carried materials did their work with one hand and held a weapon in the other, and each of the builders wore his sword at his side as he worked. But the man who sounded the trumpet stayed with me." (Nehemiah 4:16–18 NIV)

"So we continued the work with half the men holding spears, from the first light of dawn till the stars came out. At that time I also said to the people, 'Have every man and his helper stay inside Jerusalem at night, so they can serve us as guards by night and workmen by day.'" (Nehemiah 4:21–22 NIV)

※ ※ ※ ※

"WE . . . WILL KILL THEM"

"Before they know it or see us, we will be right there among them and will kill them" (Nehemiah 4:11 NIV). What Nehemiah now faced was a lot more serious than mere criticism. Sanballat threatened a surprise attack to kill the workers. That will sound familiar if you remember the 1950–1990 "cold war" years. In 1956, the Soviet premier, Nikita Khrushchev, vowed to the United States, "We will bury you!" That was not an idle threat since the Soviets were a nuclear power with both long-range bombers and ICBMs (Intercontinental Ballistic Missiles). America was dotted with signs for

Nuclear Attack Shelters, and we had nuclear attack drills in school (much more exciting than fourth-grade social studies). To avert the surprise element, the US established NORAD (North American Aerospace Defense Command), which was originally a chain of land-based radar stations in Alaska and Canada. Today, that system is augmented by the 24/7 AEWCS (Airborne Early Warning and Control System—Boeing E-3 Sentry) aircraft that can remain airborne, unrefueled, for eleven hours and can detect aircraft 250 miles away.

The risk of nuclear attack is signaled to the US Armed Forces by a five-point DEFCON (defense condition) system with DEFCON 5 meaning a "low risk" of attack and DEFCON 1 meaning an attack is "imminent." Our military has never received a DEFCON 1 signal. DEFCON 2 has been signaled only once (during the 1962 Cuban missile crisis); DEFCON 3, twice (during the 1973 Yom Kippur War in Israel and immediately after the 9/11 terrorist attacks).

NORAD and AEWCS were effective deterrents against attacks on the US homeland until Islamic terrorists hijacked four commercial aircraft and used them as flying bombs on September 11, 2001. Suddenly, we had a new "we will kill you" enemy that could not be countered with F-16 fighter jets, B-1 bombers, submarine-launched missiles, or Nimitz-class aircraft carriers. So, one year after 9/11, the Department of Homeland Security was created with a mission to "ensure a homeland that is safe, secure, and resilient against terrorism" (see DHS website, www.dhs.gov). The magnitude of their task is staggering. They must cover more than 6,000 miles of land borders and 12,000 miles of coastline, more than 6 million cargo containers entering US ports every year, and more than 700 million passengers in US airports. No wonder it takes a budget of $100 billion and 200,000 employees. The danger of a terrorist attack is signaled by the National Terrorism Advisory System (NTAS), which issues public "Imminent" or "Elevated" alerts when the risk is high. (Go to dhs.gov/alerts to find out if you should be worried as you read this.)

It is not just America that has enemies intent on destroying her; you do, too. In the business world, competition can be ruthless and can carry a "we will bury you" tone. For example, author Grant Cardone claims:

> **Kill the competition is the only way to think about your business and especially your competition . . . . In my companies we shamelessly do everything we can to eliminate and destroy competition.**[83]

Make no mistake about it, McDonald's or Wendy's would be thrilled if the other went out of business (though they would never say so publicly). Neither GM nor Ford would cry over the demise of Chrysler—or better yet, Toyota. I once had a competitor from Southeast Asia tell me that his goal was to put my company out of business. We did not become best friends, and by the way, he didn't succeed. If you are a pastor and your church is truly penetrating darkness with light, then you have a "we will kill you" enemy: "Your adversary the Devil is prowling around like a roaring lion, looking for anyone he can devour" (1 Peter 5:8 HCSB). If as a business leader or employee you are carrying light into the marketplace, the roaring lion is after you, too.

In the last chapter, Nehemiah faced passive opposition—criticism, taunting, ridicule—which attacks the heart and was intended to demoralize the workers so they would abandon the wall. It didn't work: "So we built the wall and the whole wall was joined together to half its height, for the people had a mind to work" (Nehemiah 4:6 NASB95). When criticism didn't kill the project, Sanballat and his cronies (Tobiah, the Arabs, the Ammonites, and the men of Ashdod) became "very angry" and escalated their opposition to threats of "we . . . will kill them and put an end to the work." Jerusalem was surrounded on four sides, and the threats were intended to instill fear in the workers. It did: "Then the Jews who lived near them came and told us ten times over, 'Wherever you turn, they will attack us'" (Nehemiah 4:12 NIV).

People normally react to fear in one of three ways: (1) they are frozen like a deer in the headlights and get run over; (2) they run to the nearest hiding place; or (3) they respond with determination and courage. However, before they do anything, they usually look to their leader. If the leader is weak, frozen with fear, or running away, the people are quick to follow. If the leader stands strong with determination and courage, the people will likely follow suit. This is true when your business, your church, your family, or your health is threatened. When fear creeps—or rushes—into your organization, you become the center of attention because everyone is looking to see how you will respond. So you can't ignore threats. Nehemiah couldn't; you can't.

Nehemiah had to respond to the threats of "we will kill you." What did he do first? "We prayed to our God" (Nehemiah 4:9 NIV). We have seen before that Nehemiah's first inclination in any situation was always prayer (Nehemiah 1:4, 1:5–11, 2:4, 4:4–5, 4:9, 5:19, 6:9, 6:14). We should follow Nehemiah's example. No threat is so grave or so urgent that prayer should not be our first act of response. Because there are many great books on prayer, I am not discussing it in depth here, but make no mistake about it—it is at the top of my daily leadership tool kit whether I am threatened or not. No doubt Nehemiah was familiar with and took comfort in the psalms and the prayers of King David: "Though a mighty army surrounds me, my heart will not be afraid. Even if I am attacked, I will remain confident"(Psalm 27:3 NLT).

Nehemiah was "not afraid" and was "confident." And we have the same promises he did: "For God has not given us a spirit of fearfulness, but one of power, love, and sound judgment" (2 Timothy 1:7 HCSB). Instead of fear, we can have confidence, power, and sound judgment, and guess what? God wants us to use them. So after prayer, Nehemiah didn't sit around waiting for a miracle; he went into action, using his *sound judgment* to do everything within his *power* to do.

HALFTIME ADJUSTMENTS

On November 15, 2011, Duke beat Michigan State, giving Coach K (Mike Krzyzewski) his 903rd victory—the most in NCAA Division I men's basketball history. In his worth-your-time-to-read book *Leading with the Heart*, Coach K says, "basketball is a game of adjustments—just like business."[84] In basketball, the adjustments can be to change the line-up, use a zone defense instead of the man-to-man that isn't working, call a timeout, and so on. The need for adjustments is true for basketball and business, true for churches, true for life, true for wall building. For Nehemiah, the game had changed. Building a wall from a pile of rubble was tough enough without having to worry about an arrow in the back. The wall was finished to "half its height." The second half was going to be a lot harder because of the "we will kill them" threats being shouted at the workers. Completing the wall was going to require two things: first, courage, and second, some halftime adjustments to the plan.

Courage. What is the best way for leaders to instill courage in their followers? Demonstrate it! Ancient Athenian General Laches said it 2,500 years ago: "He is a man of courage who does not run away, but remains at his post and fights against the enemy."[85]

History is full of examples of men and women who remained at their post, many sacrificing their lives. George Washington was beloved by his army because he always remained at his post. He was the "first to lead and the last to withdraw."[86] The "Texicans" at the Alamo (1836) stayed at their post and gave their lives fighting for freedom. Todd Beamer said, "Let's roll" and led a group of men on United Airlines Flight 93 to battle terrorists with their bare hands, crashing the plane into a Pennsylvania field rather than letting it hit a target in Washington, DC. In March 2012, a southern Indiana mom, Stephanie Decker, lay on top of her two children to shield them from a tornado. The kids survived unhurt; she lost both legs. Nehemiah's "remaining at his post" pre-dates them all: "Neither I nor my brothers nor my men nor the guards with me took off our clothes; each had his weapon, even when he went for water" (Nehemiah 4:23 NIV). When the workers looked around, there was Nehemiah. When they felt fear creeping in, there was Nehemiah. When they wondered "who has our backs," there was Nehemiah. And he was doing more than making speeches; he was armed and ready to fight.

As I write this, yesterday was Martin Luther King Jr. Day. To African-Americans, it is more important than July 4 (they were still slaves in 1776). In my lifetime, there has been no greater example of leadership courage than Dr. King's. On the march from Selma, Alabama, Dr. King was out front. In Birmingham, when Bull Conner turned water cannons on the marchers, Dr. King was out front. He always led from the front, knowing there was great danger: "I've seen the Promised Land. I may not get there with you . . . ."[87] He didn't—he was assassinated the day after he spoke those words.

At some point, any leader who accomplishes something significant will have to stand on the wall with courage, leading from the front. A CEO may need to pull millions of dollars of product off the shelves to ensure public safety. Johnson & Johnson did this in 1982 when they recalled 31 million bottles of Tylenol to protect the public from an unknown murderer who had laced eight bottles of Tylenol with cyanide in the Chicago area. A politician may have to cast a vote that will cost him an election. A pastor may have to exercise spiritual discipline on his church's biggest giver. A manager may have to refuse to "cook the books." A coach may have to suspend her best player for breaking team rules. Courage is essential for leadership because, as Billy Graham declares: "Courage is contagious. When a brave man takes a stand, the spines of others are often stiffened."[88]

When Nehemiah climbed up on the half-finished wall with his sword in hand, the spines of the workers were stiffened, and they were ready to keep working. Nehemiah's example, coupled with three important "halftime adjustments," gave the workers the confidence and courage they needed to stay on the job.

Adjustment #1—Early warning and alarm system. Nehemiah did not have NORAD, spy satellites, or E-3 Sentry aircraft to warn him that Sanballat was attacking. There were no citywide siren systems to sound the alarm if the Ammonites tried a surprise assault on the southern wall at dawn. Nehemiah had to do it the old-fashioned way. At strategic points around the wall, men served as watchmen with a trumpet in hand to sound the alarm in case of attack. Nehemiah "posted a guard day and night to meet this threat" (Nehemiah 4:9 NIV). And he told the watchmen exactly what to do:

> Then I said to the nobles, the officials and the rest of the people, "The work is extensive and spread out, and we are widely separated from each other along the wall. Wherever you hear the sound of the trumpet, join us there. (Nehemiah 4:19-20 NIV)

Every organization—whether a business, church, school, government, or family—needs watchmen on the wall who are looking for signs of attack, weakness, slippage, and complacency that can, by sudden eruption or slow erosion, bring down the wall. The watchmen are the ones who will tell the truth and ask the hard questions. Why are our (Blackberry) sales collapsing when everyone else's smartphone business is exploding? Why are we (Kodak) hanging onto our fading film business while digital photography is sweeping us away into bankruptcy? Why have so many young families with children left our church to attend down the street? Are we (Honda) ever going to respond to the growth of Hyundai and Kia that is shrinking our market share? Debt is my enemy; how much longer will I go before I say "enough" and get control of my family's spending? When the leader or the organization is threatened, someone has to sound the alarm. There are good reasons the apostle Paul wrote:

> Be on the alert, stand firm in the faith, act like men, be strong. (1 Corinthians 16:13 NASB95)

> Therefore let him who thinks he stands take heed that he does not fall. (1 Corinthians 10:12 NASB95)

It is the leader's job to make sure that the organization is "on the alert" and will "take heed" when the alarm sounds. Nehemiah could have ignored Sanballat, but he didn't, and you shouldn't ignore your Sanballats either. Don't let them sneak up on you.

Adjustment #2—Reinforce the weak spots. In the late 1960s and early 1970s, the Japanese auto industry attacked the two major weak spots of the US auto industry: American cars were gas guzzlers (remember *muscle cars* and long lines at the gas pump?) and the quality was poor. First, they came in with smaller, high-mpg cars and followed that with reliable, high-quality cars that seemed to last forever. Their strategy worked then and continues working today. Four of the five top-selling cars in 2011 were models from Toyota, Honda, Nissan, and Hyundai (all now made in the US). The US industry is making progress, but leads only in pickups and SUVs.

Attacking weak spots has always been a key part of battle plans. One of the earliest and still relevant books on warfare is *The Art of War*, a thirteen-chapter treatise on military strategy compiled by Chinese General Sun Tzu about 2,500 years ago. The sixth chapter concentrates on the weak and strong points of defense and says this: "You can be sure of succeeding in your attacks if you only attack places which are undefended . . . . You may advance and be absolutely irresistible, if you make for the enemy's weak points."[89]

Nehemiah did not have military training or experience, and it is very unlikely he had ever heard of *The Art of War*. However, he had no doubt overheard King Artaxerxes and his generals discuss military tactics while he kept their wine glasses full, and from that he had gleaned Sun Tzu's principles. So the second halftime adjustment he made was to pay special attention to the weakest points in the wall, the low and exposed places: "Therefore I stationed some of the people behind the lowest points of the wall at the exposed places" (Nehemiah 4:13 NIV).

There are two steps in reinforcing the weak spots: first, identifying them; second, shoring them up. For Nehemiah, both steps were easy—walk the wall, find all the low and exposed places, then station additional people there. For you, it may not be as easy, especially if your organization operates in a climate that buries the truth about itself, or about you. In any organization, the unvarnished truth about "exposed places" is essential to long-term success. If you are the leader, it is your job to expose the exposed places. In *Leadership Is an Art*, Max De Pree (former CEO of Herman Miller) says, "The first responsibility of a leader is to define reality,"[90] and part of reality is always the exposed places. If you don't know where your exposed places are, get help. And just in case *you* are the exposed place, read *The Emperor's New Clothes* to remind yourself about how really easy self-deception can be.

Adjustment #3—Show of force. With the Soviets and the United States both possessing thousands of missiles and nuclear warheads, the primary reason—maybe the only reason—the cold war never erupted into a mutually-annihilating nuclear exchange was the notion of deterrence. The Soviets had the ability to inflict massive damage on the US, but the retaliation would have been equally catastrophic. The cost to both sides wasn't worth the risk.

Nehemiah used the same tactic to deter an attack on Jerusalem. Sanballat could no doubt see the guards on the wall and the extra people in the low and exposed places. He had lost the element of surprise, and there were no easy entry points. His only option was a frontal assault—both iffy and costly. To make sure Sanballat knew exactly how costly it would be, Nehemiah's third halftime adjustment was a show of force. First, he reassigned half of the men to be full-time soldiers, fully equipped: "From that day on, half of my men did the work, while the other half were equipped with spears, shields, bows and armor" (Nehemiah 4:16 NIV). Then he created what today we would call a militia or national guard, arming everyone else who could fight: ". . . . posting them by families, with their swords, spears and bows" (Nehemiah 4:13 NIV). So when Sanballat looked at the wall, he saw not just a few guards with trumpets, but hundreds of armed men, fully ready to stave off any attack at any time.

Whereas today when we mobilize the National Guard it takes days, Nehemiah's militia was one trumpet blast away from dropping their picks and shovels; picking up their *swords, spears, and bows*; and joining the fight within minutes. The element of surprise was lost. The weak spots were strengthened. The people were armed and ready to fight. Nehemiah, without an arrow fired, achieved what General Sun Tzu called "supreme excellence": "To fight and conquer in all our battles is not supreme excellence; supreme excellence consists in breaking the enemy's resistance without fighting."[91]

Knowing that the cost to attack would be very high, Sanballat dropped the idea altogether. The enemies' resistance was broken without fighting. Of course, Nehemiah did what he always did; he gave the credit to God: "When our enemies heard that we were aware of their plot and that *God had frustrated it* . . . . " (Nehemiah 4:15 NIV, emphasis mine).

CIRCLE THE WAGONS

As a boy growing up in Oklahoma, there wasn't much I liked more than an Indians versus wagon train movie, especially if John Wayne was the one who led the charge to rescue the wagon train. (Of course, this means my favorite movies and TV shows are more than fifty years old and often in black and white.) When evening came after a hot, dry day on the trail, ever alert for hostiles, they would "circle the wagons" so they could sit around the campfires, eat a gourmet meal cooked by somebody named Sagebrush, and sing songs about the prairie while they gazed at the stars. Then it was off to bed for a night of sweet dreams about how wonderful California was going to be. Well . . . that's what they did in the movies. The circled wagons were a respite from constant danger—a place of safety that took the edge off of the fear that hovered over the trail every day.

Because living under constant threat takes a physical and emotional toll, people need a break, a time when they can feel safe—or at least safer—so they can rest and replenish their bodies and spirits. People are especially vulnerable when they are tired or afraid. After a long day working on the wall and watching over their shoulders for an attack that could come at any time, Nehemiah's people needed a break. They needed to circle the wagons, so Nehemiah said to the people, "Have every man and his helper stay inside Jerusalem at night, so they can serve us as guards by night and workmen by day" (Nehemiah 4:22 NIV). While working on the wall, they were exposed, but inside the walls they could relax a bit, knowing the guards were on duty, constantly ready to blow the trumpet.

A wise leader knows when it is time to circle the wagons so followers can relax, take a break, and feel safe, at least for a while. Circling the wagons takes many forms depending on the threat, need, and type of organization. As the leader, you will have to decide what it looks like for your followers. For example, in addition to fear, Nehemiah's workers were tired and discouraged: "Meanwhile, the people in Judah said, 'The strength of the laborers is giving out, and there is so much rubble that we cannot rebuild the wall'" (Nehemiah 4:10 NIV). For his tired and discouraged workers, Nehemiah circled the wagons, after which they *all returned to the wall, each to his own work"* (Nehemiah 4:15 NIV, emphasis mine).

If you aren't sure what to do, ask. Your followers will know what will best take the pressure off and reduce the fear for them. And hopefully, you aren't the one creating the fear. If you are, the sooner you find out the better.

THE ROARING LION

When the attack is from the roaring lion . . .

> Your adversary the Devil is prowling around like a roaring lion,
> looking for anyone he can devour. (1 Peter 5:8 HCSB)

and sooner or later it will be, there are specific scriptures that are much more
helpful than anything I can say:

> Resist the devil, and he will flee from you. (James 4:7 NIV)

> Put on the full armor of God so that you can take your stand against
> the devil's schemes. (Ephesians 6:11 NIV)

> Be alert, stand firm in the faith, be brave and strong. (1 Corinthians
> 16:13 HCSB)

And this final scripture deserves special attention:

> By yourself you're unprotected. With a friend you can face the worst.
> Can you round up a third? A three-stranded rope isn't easily snapped.
> (Ecclesiastes 4:12 *The Message*)

Don't resist the roaring lion alone. Get help!

Leadership **11** **BE ALERT, BE ARMED,**
STONE **BE READY TO FIGHT.**

Responding aggressively to threats, with courage and flexibility, is a
crucial part of a leader's job description. When your organization is under
attack, you can't just sit back, act like it isn't happening, and hope for the
best. Moving half of the men from working on the wall to defending the wall
was a big change in Nehemiah's construction plan. I'm sure he was reluctant
to do it because the shift would slow progress on the wall.

Leaders face situations like this all the time. A new competitor becomes
a threat; technology becomes obsolete almost overnight; key staff members
retire or move on to new opportunities; capital campaigns flop. Effective
leaders are alert for changing circumstances, and they respond appropriately.

There is a saying in the military that battle plans are good until the first shot is fired. Nehemiah's plan was good until Sanballat said, "We will kill them." Then, it had to change—a lot!

Are you standing on the wall with courage and a stiff back?

Do your people know you have their backs?

Are you alert and watching for threats to your organization? Who is watching with you?

When the alarm sounds, will you listen?

What adjustments do you need to make?

What armor and show of force will deter your enemies?

Is it time for you to circle the wagons? Do your people need a break? Do you?

Are you in a fight with the roaring lion? Who is helping you?

As the leader, "homeland security" is up to you. The safety of your company, your church, or your family is your responsibility: "When a strong man, armed to the teeth, stands guard in his front yard, his property is safe and sound" (Luke 11:21 *The Message*). Your job is to be strong and courageous: a strong leader, strong pastor, strong parent—alert, armed, and *ready to fight.* ◼

12

CLASS WARFARE

Perquisites and deferences create a protective cocoon—
if not a full-fledged fantasy world—
for the chieftains of some of the nation's largest companies.[92]

BUSINESSWEEK

It's hard enough to finish this wall with enemies lurking around threatening to attack us, but now we have problems inside the walls, too. The last thing Nehemiah needs is a lot of disgruntled Jews, but he's got them. A delegation of workers came to see him yesterday with a long list of grievances. The famine has pushed them over the edge. It has shrunk the harvest so much that they are mortgaging their fields and even selling their children into slavery to get money to buy grain so they can eat. And the ridiculously high taxes aren't helping matters either. Worse yet, our own leaders, the Jewish nobles and officials, are party to this. They are taking advantage of the situation by charging high interest rates that can't be repaid, then foreclosing on the farms the first chance they get.

Nehemiah is livid about this whole thing. He told me last night he's afraid it could sink the wall project. Not to mention that it's just plain wrong and they know better. So this morning, he got right in the face of the offenders and read them the riot act. At first they were speechless, but then they began to backtrack and promised to make it right. Nehemiah made them take an oath, with the priests as witnesses, so they wouldn't get amnesia in a few weeks. By this afternoon, everyone had calmed down and gone back to work.

His face-off with the nobility crowd is why the people trust Nehemiah so much. He doesn't lord it over them and even takes their side in a conflict when he knows they're right.

One of the greatest things about Nehemiah is that he leads by example and doesn't take advantage of his position as governor. He is paying for all the meals he serves—more than 150 on most days—out of his own pocket, and hasn't bought any land for his own benefit. He has postponed building a governor's mansion until the walls are finished and all the people are safe and back to their normal life. Every governor before him took care of himself first—usually at the expense of the people—but Nehemiah just won't do it. I've asked him about it, and all he says is, "I'm here to serve them, not the other way around." It's no wonder the people respect him so much and so readily follow his leadership.

NEHEMIAH'S JOURNAL

"Now the men and their wives raised a great outcry against their Jewish brothers. Some were saying, 'We and our sons and daughters are numerous; in order for us to eat and stay alive, we must get grain.' Others were saying, 'We are mortgaging our fields, our vineyards and our homes to get grain during the famine.' Still others were saying, 'We have had to borrow money to pay the king's tax on our fields and vineyards. Although we are of the same flesh and blood as our countrymen and though our sons are as good as theirs, yet we have to subject our sons and daughters to slavery. Some of our daughters have already been enslaved, but we are powerless, because our fields and our vineyards belong to others.' When I heard their outcry and these charges, I was very angry. I pondered them in my mind and then accused the nobles and officials. I told them, 'You are exacting usury from your own countrymen!' So I called together a large meeting to deal with them and said: 'As far as possible, we have bought back our Jewish brothers who were sold to the Gentiles. Now you are selling your brothers, only for them to be sold back to us!' They kept quiet, because they could find nothing to say. So I continued, 'What you are doing is not right. Shouldn't you walk in the fear of our God to avoid the reproach of our Gentile enemies? I and my brothers and my men are also lending the people money and grain. But let the exacting of usury stop! Give back to them immediately their fields, vineyards, olive groves and houses, and also the usury you are charging them—the hundredth part of the

money, grain, new wine and oil.' 'We will give it back,' they said. 'And we will not demand anything more from them. We will do as you say.' Then I summoned the priests and made the nobles and officials take an oath to do what they had promised." (Nehemiah 5:1–12 NIV)

##

THAT COULD NEVER HAPPEN HERE . . . COULD IT?

The "great outcry" that reached Nehemiah's ears was serious. It threatened to split the workers and stop or slow the work on the wall. Under a heavy load of taxes imposed by the government, usurious interest rates imposed by rich lenders, and a famine that depleted the supply of grain, the middle and lower classes were "mortgaging our fields." They had to borrow "money to pay the king's tax" and subject their "sons and daughters to slavery." They felt "powerless, because our fields and our vineyards belong to others."

Don't dismiss this chapter, assuming this kind of economic slavery can't happen anymore. It can and has within the last century—even in America.

In the spring of 1912, a "great outcry" arose from the miners who worked the fifty-five Paint Creek and Cabin Creek coal mines in West Virginia. More than 7500 miners went on strike because they were virtual slaves to the coal companies. They lived in company-owned housing, paying rent set by the companies. The tools and equipment they used were company-owned, leased at rates set by the company. To make matters worse, they weren't paid wages in dollars, but in company-issued scrip that could only be used in company-owned stores where the prices were set by . . . you guessed it . . . the company. When they were able to win pay increases, the company got the money back by simply raising the prices for housing, tools, and food. Stranded in remote valleys with no money and little if any education, the miners seemingly had no way out. Their cry was the same one Nehemiah heard: "We have to subject our sons and daughters to slavery." Change did not come quickly or easily for the miners. More than twenty years of strikes and violence, hundreds of deaths, military intervention, and new laws were needed before they won some semblance of freedom and dignity. (Read *Bloodletting in Appalachia* by Howard B. Lee to get the full, sad story.)

In the mid-fifties, my brothers used to earn pocket money by picking cotton in southwest Oklahoma for about a nickel or dime a pound. Until the fifties, a lot of cotton in the south was produced by another form of economic slavery: sharecropping. In the years before World War II, more than half of all farmers—black and white—were landless, meaning they farmed (usually cotton, sometimes tobacco) somebody else's land for a share of the profit. Since they had to borrow to buy seed, fertilizer, etc., at interest rates set by the landowner, and since drought, floods, boll weevils, and other maladies often reduced the yield, sharecroppers were trapped in a system they could not escape. Not until machinery became the most efficient way to plant, weed, and harvest cotton on large corporate-owned farms did the sharecropper system begin to dissipate. Although it openly persisted into the 1990s on California strawberry farms, today it is largely an underground economic activity, hidden from view, but still insidious and enslaving for some.

Nehemiah was not the first leader, nor the last, to hear the "great outcry" of workers who are oppressed—or think they are. From the very first time one shepherd had two sheep while his neighbor had only one, the sounds of class warfare—real or imagined—have assaulted the ears of leaders. I am writing this chapter in January 2012, a presidential election year. Cries of class warfare are being launched against the Democrats because they want to raise taxes on the rich and against the Republicans because they are opposed, believing that higher taxes will hurt the economy. Class warfare is alleged in union versus company disputes, in salaried versus hourly squabbles, and in the Wall Street versus Main Street debate. Class warfare can arise in a church if the lead pastor elevates himself or in a car dealership when the sales staff derides the service department. In some cases, private versus public education takes on tones of class warfare. A haughty headquarters staff can launch a class war in any company or organization. Voiced or not, it probably exists to some degree in your organization, whether it is a business, church, or government agency. So although the specifics of the complaints Nehemiah heard were different from what leaders hear today, the root causes were much the same.

THE SEEDS OF CLASS WARFARE

Some of what I am about to say is going to upset some of you. You may be offended or angered, but I hope not. My only intent is to stimulate your thinking about what you can do to mitigate the risk of class warfare charges in the organization you lead, because the danger is real.

If you feel that I am unfairly charging you with class warfare, let me soften the blow a bit. Nehemiah was confronted with charges that the rich *nobles and officials* were oppressing the poor. In Nehemiah's case, the charges were true. They may not be true in your case, but it is possible—even probable—that you will still encounter the charges of it. In the eyes of the receptionist, the cleaning crew, the cafeteria worker, and the nursery diaper-changer, the CEO, manager, principal, and megachurch senior pastor are the rich nobles and officials of today. So that is the perspective I am taking in this chapter. I am not declaring anyone guilty, but I am suggesting that a view "from the floor" is a good thing every now and then.

Are there other seeds of class warfare besides the nature of your position? Oh, yes. For example, I grew up in a no-stoplight, southwest Oklahoma town of about 1,000 people. Trust me, it was not a quaint little haven for artists and retired CEOs; we had no—absolutely zero!—rich nobles and officials in our town. However, that didn't stop us from elevating ourselves whenever we had the chance. About five miles east was a "hick" town of about 100 people. And guess what? We actually looked down our noses at them, thinking, *How can they stand to live in a cruddy little place like that?* Of course, the 10,000 people who lived in the county seat fifteen miles to the northwest felt exactly the same way about us.

I do not claim to be an expert or have all the answers to the class warfare issue. However, I have led large organizations—union and nonunion—that struggled with underlying currents of class warfare that distracted from the work, hurt morale, and undermined productivity. I learned there is no way to eliminate it entirely, but there are things you can do to lessen the clamor and the damage. I have seen the roots of class warfare sprout and flourish in environments where the leaders are driven by greed or when leaders catch CEO Disease, afflicted by the four Ps—power, privilege, possessions, and pride.

Greed. The great outcry Nehemiah heard had its roots in greed and in a sense of entitlement that is common with "nobles and officials." The oppressors didn't care that their own greed was enslaving their brothers. When Nehemiah confronted them, they had no defense: "They kept quiet, because they could find nothing to say" (Nehemiah 5:8 NIV). Then, Nehemiah challenged them further with, "Shouldn't you walk in the fear of our God?" (Nehemiah 5:9 NIV). They were guilty, and they knew it. To their credit, they responded with, "We will give it back . . . we will not demand anything more from them" (Nehemiah 5:12 NIV).

As a leader—especially if you are a Christian—it is your responsibility to "walk in the fear of the Lord" and make sure that greed—yours or others'—is not driving a wedge of division in your organization. Leaders work hard and carry the mantle of heavy responsibility. Their decisions affect the livelihood and future of their people, whether a few or thousands. As a result, leaders should be rewarded the most—few dispute that—but they should also remember that "the love of money is a root of all kinds of evil" (1 Timothy 6:10 HCSB). "All kinds of evil" takes many forms. In extreme cases, the love of money has put people in jail (e.g., Bernie Madoff, Bernie Ebbers, and Dennis Kozlowski).

In American corporate life, the love of money has created a system of reward in which the CEOs of the top 500 public companies were paid an average of about $9 million per year in 2010—about 150 times as much as a typical American working family. No doubt, many of these executives deserved every penny. However, this pay gap is a major point of debate in our nation, and to close it, some people believe income redistribution is the solution (I don't). The truth is, even if these CEOs were paid nothing, and the dollars were redistributed to all their employees, it would add only a few hundred dollars per year to the income of a typical employee in those companies. And if the money were redistributed to every person in the United States, it would be less than $20 apiece. Further, if the federal government taxed away 100 percent of the top 500 CEOs' income, it would eliminate less than two days' worth of the country's 2012-level deficit!

Now, please don't misunderstand me. Leaders should be the highest paid employees in an organization. I know from personal experience how difficult and demanding a C-Level job is. I know firsthand the exhausting travel and unrelenting pressure of making the numbers every month. The job demands are high, so the rewards should be high. However, there is a point where enough is enough, and it is impossible to avoid charges of class warfare when a CEO or any leader makes more in one year than an average family makes in three or four *lifetimes*. Is it really just greed? According to Dane Miller, the former CEO of Biomet, the answer is yes: "What incremental value does an extra 100,000 shares have? At some point, you're just satisfying an uncontrollable greed complex."[93]

Let me clarify that controversies about executive pay are usually focused on "compensation for services," which is the pay that employees—executives and otherwise—receive as employees of an organization. An altogether different matter is "compensation for ownership," which arises from starting or buying a business, building it or rebuilding it, and eventually selling all or part of it for a substantial gain. Success in business ownership is good old-fashioned American capitalism at work. It is the reward—based on the market value of the enterprise—for entrepreneurial risk taking. A real-life example of this is Hamdi Ulukaya and the Chobani Greek Yogurt story. Ulukaya, a Turkish immigrant, bought a "going out of business" yogurt factory in New York, and in just four years (2007–2011) built the business into a $700-million-per-year-and-still-growing enterprise. At some point in the future, he will no doubt reap the (huge) rewards of his risk taking and hard work and will deserve every penny—*no matter how much it is.*

In no way does God disapprove of us making money—even a lot of money. However, he does not approve when our primary motive is to build bigger barns:

> **And he [Jesus] told them this parable: "The ground of a certain rich man produced a good crop. He thought to himself, 'What shall I do? I have no place to store my crops.' Then he said, 'This is what I'll do. I will tear down my barns and build bigger ones, and there I will store all my grain and my goods. And I'll say to myself, "You have plenty of good things laid up for many years. Take life easy; eat, drink and be merry." ' But God said to him, 'You fool! This very night your life will be demanded from you. Then who will get what you have prepared for yourself?'" (Luke 12:16-21 NIV)**

God also warns against making money by taking advantage of our employees:

> **Never take advantage of poor and destitute laborers, whether they are fellow Israelites or foreigners living in your towns. You must pay them their wages each day before sunset because they are poor and are counting on it. (Deuteronomy 24:14–15 NLT)**

If charges of class warfare are raised in your organization, make sure it is not because of greedy leadership—yours or anyone else's.

CEO Disease. 4P leaders who believe their positions are about power, privilege, possessions, and pride are sure to have an undercurrent of class warfare in their organizations. A 1991 *Businessweek* article referred to 4P leaders as having "CEO Disease." One of them "ruled over his company as if it were a private fiefdom."[94] A 4P leader will often "compete with industry counterparts over how much money he makes, how big the headquarters building is, or how many corporate jets are parked on the landing strip."[95] But does focusing on such things really matter all that much? Yes. The article went on to say: "Much of the damage done by an afflicted CEO is insidious, striking at the heart of the corporation's ability to compete: employee morale."[96]

Has anything changed since 1991? Not much. It is a rare week when the *Wall Street Journal* does not have at least one story about a 4P business leader using his or her company as a "private fiefdom."

Sadly, CEO Disease has even spread into some churches, where 4P pastors set their own rules and impose heavy burdens on everyone else, especially their staffs. They too often fit Jesus' description of religious leaders who "tie up heavy loads and put them on men's shoulders, but they themselves are not willing to lift a finger to move them" (Matthew 23:4 NIV). Tests of "loyalty" often mean keeping quiet, and if you don't . . . well, watch your back.

All of us, business and ministry leaders alike, would do well to remember and follow the charge of Peter: "Don't lord it over the people assigned to your care, but lead them by your own good example" (1 Peter 5:3 NLT).

IT'S NOT ABOUT YOU

The first sentence in Rick Warren's mega-selling (40+ million copies) book, *The Purpose Driven Life*, is "It's not about you."[97] A great starting point for minimizing class warfare in your organization is to remember that as the leader, IT IS NOT ABOUT YOU. Few have expressed this more powerfully and concisely than Peter Drucker: "Rank does not confer privilege or give power. It imposes responsibility."[98] Should it matter to you what Peter Drucker has to say? Yes. Upon his death in 2005, *Businessweek* dubbed him *The Man Who Invented Management*[99] and GE's former CEO, Jack Welch, called him "the greatest management thinker of the last century."[100] Both greed and CEO Disease arise in a heart focused on self. I know well the "look at what I've accomplished" temptation.

My first job in corporate life was with a defense company. For security reasons, everyone wore a badge at all times, even the company president. So that everyone would know your "rank" in the company, all the badges had color bars. There was one color for union employees, a different color for office hourly, still another for office salaried. There were colors for professionals and colors for security clearances. Some badges had two or three colors. As an engineer, my deepest desire was to get a blue badge, which let everyone know I was more important and higher paid than engineers with green badges, and would also, by the way, get me a numbered parking place in a lot near my office.

After receiving my blue badge and parking spot, my next goal was to have my own cubicle, after which I went for a real office, then a parking place with my name on it, followed by lunch privileges in the management dining room. Then came the big day when my name was added to the bonus list, and not long after came a company car and office on the executive hallway. Of course, once on that hallway, what I wanted was an office with a personal bathroom, and finally the corner office. I got it, and once there, CEO Disease began to take hold. I allowed myself way too many "look at what I've done" days. After five years "at the top," I was replaced for complex business reasons, but mostly it was God protecting me from myself by reminding me to "let him who thinks he stands take heed that he does not fall" (1 Corinthians 10:12 NASB95).

It was a bruising—but necessary—blow. Didn't Jesus say something like "whoever exalts himself shall be humbled"? In the weeks after, I asked Dottie, "How has this affected me?" Her response was, "I think you are more humble." And I needed to be. Enough said.

There is no better example of IT'S NOT ABOUT YOU than Nehemiah:

> Moreover . . . when I was appointed to be their governor in the land
> of Judah . . . neither I nor my brothers ate the food allotted to the
> governor. But the earlier governors—those preceding me—placed a
> heavy burden on the people and took forty shekels of silver from them
> in addition to food and wine. Their assistants also lorded it over the
> people. But out of reverence for God I did not act like that. Instead, I
> devoted myself to the work on this wall. All my men were assembled
> there for the work; we did not acquire any land. Furthermore, a hun-
> dred and fifty Jews and officials ate at my table, as well as those who

came to us from the surrounding nations . . . . In spite of all this, I never demanded the food allotted to the governor, because the demands were heavy on these people. Remember me with favor, O my God, for all I have done for these people. (Nehemiah 5:14–19 NIV)

Keep in mind that Nehemiah was the governor of Judah appointed by King Artaxerxes. He had the power to do most anything he wanted to do. It was definitely an it's-all-about-me position, highly vulnerable to CEO Disease. But what did he do? "Out of reverence for God I did not act like that." When Peter wrote that leaders *should not* "lord it over the people assigned to your care," he went on to say what we *should* do: "lead them by your own good example" (1 Peter 5:3 NLT). Nehemiah did it right.

GET RID OF THE BLUE BADGES

Much of the outcry and charges of class warfare arise from visible things that divide people or set some people apart. There is no way to completely eliminate these things, and even if you could, there would still be charges of class warfare from some individuals or groups. There is nothing—absolutely nothing—you can do that will satisfy everyone and seem fair to everyone. In spite of the complete failure of communism and socialism, there are still those who believe everyone should be paid the same, have the same size office, and so on. So don't try to score 100 on this—you can't. However, do make sure that the things that divide are really necessary and are not extreme. If I were leading a company today, there are a lot of things I would do differently than I did—some you may not agree with. But here they are.

Badges. Color-coded badges are an example of something that can divide unnecessarily. If you really want the cleaning crew to believe they are important and essential to your organization's success, don't send a message that they are less important than the engineers, who get a blue badge instead of a brown one. When I served on the staff of my church, I wore a name tag on Sundays that let everyone know I was the EXECUTIVE PASTOR, not one of the ordinary pastors. Yuck! STAFF would have been enough.

Parking. I remember when I arrived in Nashville for a new job, how important I felt when I got a reserved parking place with my name displayed. A reserved spot with your name signaled that you were "upper" management. Without a named, reserved spot, you were "lower" management, or worse, not management at all. Wisely, our president eventually got rid of named parking spots. The company didn't fall apart, and the "upper" people didn't leave. Actually, we were more unified.

Offices. Appropriate office arrangements have been debated for years. Companies have tried everything: no offices at all, glass-wall offices, same size offices, cubicles for everyone, and more. I can't say what is best for your organization, but keep these points in mind:

- Few things are a more potentially divisive status symbol than offices.
- Few things retard communication and spontaneous interactions more than offices.
- Few things isolate and make for better hiding places than offices.

Offices are necessary in most organizations, so be fair, be reasonable, and remember that offices are a place to work, not a showcase for your or anybody else's ego or ethos. My final point on offices is that with few exceptions—very few—nobody needs a private bathroom. Do you really want to send a message that you're too good to use the same bathroom as everyone else? (I told you I was going to make some of you mad.)

Executive suites. There is very little that divides and sends more of a class warfare message than a restricted-access executive office suite or hallway. When I arrived in Nashville, the company had a long dark 1940s style "mahogany row." It was separated from the factory by a sign on the door: OFFICES. In other words, "Don't enter unless summoned"—like when you were in junior high school. Fortunately, our change-for-the-better-oriented president got rid of the sign, and although we didn't spend the money to get rid of mahogany row (prohibitively expensive because of so much asbestos in the walls, ceilings, etc.), he did mandate that our office doors were to be open at all times unless we were having a truly confidential conversation. It is surprising how such a simple thing changed the look of the hallway from a "restricted area" to just another hallway where the president happens to spend his time.

Dining rooms. Isn't it great to go to lunch in a private upper-management-only dining room so you can talk business without interruption, especially if the cost is subsidized by the company? Actually, by lunch time I needed a break from the people I had spent the morning with. We got rid of our dining room in Nashville, and not one bad thing happened. The company saved money, and another thing that divides was removed. When we had customers in, we discovered that catering was just as easy and actually less costly in the long run. This may not be the correct move for everyone—especially if you have a parade of customers every day—but at least consider it. (By the way, a much better use of lunchtime is to brownbag with the troops on a regular basis. Try it; you'll like it.)

Company cars. When I first became a vice-president, I got the big perquisite everyone wants—a company car! It came with my job not because I used it for miles and miles of company business, but simply because I was an executive. Think about this: companies—presumably for recruiting and retention reasons—provide cars to the highest paid people who can already afford them. Few things send a "divide" signal more than company cars that aren't needed for company travel. In Nashville, we got rid of them for everyone except the president. And guess what? Not a single executive left because another company offered him a car. If you can't afford to pay your executives enough so they can have a car that doesn't embarrass you in the parking lot, how can you afford to give them a company car? (I do understand that if you have executives, or anyone, who drive a lot of company-specific mileage, a car may be appropriate. I'll let you decide what "a lot" means.)

Head tables. In talking about the religious leaders of his time, Jesus said they "love to be noticed . . . They love the place of honor at banquets and the chief seats in the synagogues" (Matthew 23:5–6 NASB95). In view of that, instead of asking, "Who should sit at the head table?" maybe we should be asking, "Do we even need a head table?" The answer can often be "no." Unless you have an outside guest who would be offended without one, you don't need a head table for company or church functions. Go sit with the engineers for a change. You won't understand a word they say, but they'll love having you. Look around for someone who is alone or seems out of place—sit with her. For crying out loud, when it's your turn to speak, it's only a five- or ten-second walk to the podium. The exercise will be good for you.

Look around. Unless you are unusual, your organization has visible things that unnecessarily divide and promote a class warfare climate. I could ramble on with a list of things for you to think about, but it will be more productive if you tackle that yourself. It won't be easy because some of the things that divide people are things you believe you've earned. Plus, everyone else is doing it. It is hard to take a position like Max De Pree's when he was at Herman Miller, Inc., that limited the CEO's pay to 20 times a factory worker's pay (from *Leadership Jazz* by Max De Pree[101]) when all around you, your peers are taking home 50 times, 100 times, or even 150 times. (At Whole Foods, by contrast, it's limited to 19 times.) And when you love Ms. Lucy's pecan pie in the executive dining room, who wants to give that up to eat in the all-hands cafeteria? This is the hard part of leadership—putting the welfare of the organization and its people above your personal welfare and preferences. So remember: it's not about you. Look around, and get rid of the blue badges and whatever else may be dividing people.

Leadership STONE 12 NO GREED OR EGO ALLOWED

Leadership is a perilous thing because it can give wings to our worst proclivities. Unless we carefully guard our hearts and minds, greed and CEO Disease will lead down a dangerous path for ourselves and our organizations. What we do as leaders will either promote a climate of class warfare or take the edge off of it. When Nehemiah was faced with charges of class warfare, he didn't hesitate to confront it: "What you are doing is not right." As a twenty-first century leader, you may need to confront it, too. Starting with IT'S NOT ABOUT YOU:

Do not think of yourself more highly than you ought. (Romans 12:3 NIV)

Don't lord it over the people assigned to your care, but lead them by your own good example. (1 Peter 5:3 NLT)

Follow Nehemiah's example. Don't take advantage of your people, and don't put heavy burdens on them so you can live the good life.

Have you let success and the mores of our culture trigger greed in your thinking and actions?

Have you forgotten that "much will be required of everyone who has been given much. And even more will be expected of the one who has been entrusted with more" (Luke 12:48 HCSB)?

Do you have a bad—or even slight—case of CEO Disease?

Are you a 4P leader? Not sure? Ask someone you trust to tell you the truth.

Are there things in your organization that unnecessarily cause division and charges of class warfare?

Are you willing to give up those things?

Is your system of rewards and privileges fair and appropriate?

Do the rules apply to everyone, or are a few favorites exempted?

Whatever the answer to these questions today, the answer can be different tomorrow if you are willing to become a leader who unites, not one who divides. Why don't you get started?

Need a contemporary example? There is none better than Max De Pree. Put *Leadership Jazz* and *Leadership Is an Art* on your "must" reading list. ▪

13

THE RED ZONE

Most people give up just when they're about to achieve success.
They quit on the one yard line. They give up at the
last minute of the game, one foot from a winning touchdown.[102]

ROSS PEROT

The last few days have been really hard on Nehemiah. The closer we get to finishing, the harder our enemies seem to work at stopping us. We're just a few days from completing the wall (hard to believe!), and Sanballat has resorted to dirty tricks and attack ads.

Sanballat's first trick was to ask Nehemiah to meet him outside of the city so they could "talk." Nehemiah didn't buy that line even though Sanballat tried four different times to coax him into the open. When that didn't work, he cranked up the rumor mill. He accused Nehemiah of planning to rebel against King Artaxerxes and declare himself king of Judah. Fortunately, everyone saw right through that one, and it didn't even get off the ground. Everyone knows Nehemiah is a man of integrity. He's 100 percent loyal to the king and has no intention of betraying him.

Speaking of betraying, I was stunned when it came out that Shemaiah was working for Tobiah and Sanballat. Shemaiah tried to convince Nehemiah he would be safe from attack by taking refuge in the inner courts of the temple where only the priests are allowed. Nehemiah blew him off. He told him, "I'm not going to run, and I'm not going to sin." He has more determination than anyone I've ever known. Nothing distracts or deters him from the task at hand. I believe he would finish the wall by himself if he had to!

*I don't know what Sanballat & Company might try next, but we'll be finished
with the wall as soon as we hang the gates—sometime in the next day or two!
Wow! It will be party time then!*

*"When word came to Sanballat, Tobiah, Geshem the Arab and the rest of our
enemies that I had rebuilt the wall and not a gap was left in it—though up to
that time I had not set the doors in the gates—Sanballat and Geshem sent me
this message: 'Come, let us meet together in one of the villages on the plain of
Ono.' But they were scheming to harm me; so I sent messengers to them with
this reply: 'I am carrying on a great project and cannot go down. Why should
the work stop while I leave it and go down to you?' Four times they sent me
the same message, and each time I gave them the same answer." (Nehemiah
6:1–4 NIV)*

THE LAST TWENTY YARDS ARE THE TOUGHEST

In American football, one of the most examined topics is the Red
Zone—that area of the field from the twenty-yard line to the goal. All of
the talking heads on TV pontificate about how important it is to score when
in the Red Zone. "You have to come away with points," they say. Or when
talking about defense, you'll hear something like, "This team may bend in
the middle of the field, but they don't break in the Red Zone." Of course,
the offense is always trying to score a touchdown, so when they stall out
and settle for a field goal, the expert analysis is, "That is going to cost them
later in the game." The average success rate (defined by actually scoring a
touchdown) for NFL teams in the Red Zone is about 50 percent. A 50 percent success ratio doesn't sound too hot. Could your organization survive
with that level of success?

Why is it so hard to finish the drive and score a touchdown in the Red
Zone? Because the closer a team gets to the goal, the more the defense digs
in to stop them. A twenty-yard play at midfield doesn't give up points. A
twenty-yard play in the Red Zone puts six points on the board, so defenses

tighten up and play harder. The Patriots were a great example of this in the 2011 season. In terms of total yards allowed, the Patriots were terrible—next to last, thirty-first out of thirty-two teams. They gave up a lot of yards. However, in terms of points allowed, they ranked a much better fifteenth. That's because in the Red Zone, they were tough.

In football, it is "finish the drive." In track and field, it is "run to the tape." A guitar player is supposed to "play until the last string breaks." Every type of endeavor has a Red Zone, close to the goal, but not there yet. The job of leaders is to lead all the way to the finish line, not stopping short, leaving nothing undone. That is not easy because opponents fight back, fatigue makes it hard to carry on, and complacency or overconfidence may set in when the goal line is in sight. Leaders can also be distracted by focusing on the next big thing before the current big thing is closed out. Too often, organizations bog down and settle for a field goal.

Nehemiah faced the same Red Zone challenges that leaders face today: "I had rebuilt the wall and not a gap was left in it—though up to that time I had not set the doors in the gates" (Nehemiah 6:1 NIV). Nehemiah's team is inside the five-yard line, on the verge of scoring, and what happens? Sanballat makes a last ditch effort to scuttle the project by using dirty tricks and nasty rumors. Even worse, a Benedict Arnold surfaces, intent on stopping Nehemiah. Those last twenty yards didn't come easily for Nehemiah. They won't for you. (Oh well, so much for getting home early.)

DIRTY TRICKS

I am writing this chapter in an election year (2012). If it is like most election years, it will be surprising if there are not a few dirty tricks. Sadly, they are part of America's election history all the way back to 1800 when Thomas Jefferson and John Adams (the incumbent) squared off in a bitter battle for the presidency. Adams' supporters (without his knowledge) started a rumor that Jefferson was dead. The rumor was widespread and was printed in many newspapers, which were the primary means of communication at that time. Actually, Thomas Jefferson, one of the slaves at Monticello, was dead. Thomas Jefferson the candidate was alive and well. (By the way, the trick didn't work—Jefferson won.) Watergate is the classic worst-ever political dirty trick. It brought down Nixon's presidency and sent four men to prison. Charges of buying votes and stuffing or losing ballot boxes occur in every election. That is why Billy Graham said correctly that "Everybody has a little bit of Watergate in him."[103]

Sanballat's plan to stop the work by storming the half-finished walls and killing the workers didn't pan out, and since he couldn't get to Nehemiah inside the walls, his next tactic was to trick Nehemiah into coming out. "Come, let us meet together" was supposed to sound like a peace offering. History is full of tragic consequences when leaders were taken in by a false lure of peace. Neville Chamberlain (prime minister of Great Britain in the years leading up to World War II) was snagged by Hitler's dirty trick in 1938 when he signed the Munich Agreement, "symbolic of the desire of our two people never to go to war again."[104] Hitler duped Chamberlain. The German leader's intent wasn't peace but simply buying more time to build up his military before taking on the British. Chamberlain's famous quote that the agreement assured "peace for our time" disintegrated a year later when Hitler invaded Poland, starting a war that consumed the world and took more than 50 million lives (more than 20 million military; more than 30 million civilian). Nehemiah was not a Neville Chamberlain and knew that any overture from Sanballat should be considered with caution. He recognized Sanballat's offer for what it was—a dirty trick: "They were scheming to harm me."

Leaders do well when they remember that not everyone has their best interests at heart. I am not suggesting that you view everyone with distrust, but do be wary and discerning, as Jesus was:

> While He was in Jerusalem at the Passover Festival, many trusted in His name when they saw the signs He was doing. Jesus, however, would not entrust Himself to them, since He knew them all. (John 2:23–24 HCSB)

Jesus similarly warned us to be shrewd and to beware of the wolves:

> "Behold, I send you out as sheep in the midst of wolves; so be shrewd as serpents and innocent as doves. But beware of men." (Matthew 10:16–17 NASB95)

When, as a leader, you are offered an olive branch from an unexpected source, do not automatically discard it, nor automatically accept it. First, make sure there isn't a "dirty trick" wolf under the sheepskin.

ATTACK ADS

I saw the first one yesterday, February 4, 2012. The primary elections are a month away in Tennessee, so the attack ads have ramped up. Some are blatantly untrue; others are half-truths presented in a way that misleads. Whereas dirty tricks are intended to manipulate the vote, attack ads are intended to manipulate the voter. In America's earliest elections, newspapers were full of them. Today it is television. Sadly, they have become the chief means of political advertising, but according to former president Bill Clinton, it doesn't matter: "People really don't care if politicians attack each other with untrue stories. They figure if you don't want to get hurt, you shouldn't have filed for office."[105]

Politics is often referred to as a "contact sport." I suspect if our founding fathers saw the sad state of politics today, they would conclude that "taxation without representation" isn't so bad. Putting it in a way only he could, Will Rogers said, "I bet after seeing us today, George Washington would sue us for calling him the 'father of our nation.'"[106]

If criticism (chapter 10) is like throwing rocks at leaders, attacks ads are like dropping bombs. Nehemiah had to reckon with both. When Sanballat's dirty trick failed to draw Nehemiah out, he pitched a "dirty bomb" over the wall:

> Sanballat sent his aide to me with the same message, and in his hand was an unsealed letter in which was written: "It is reported among the nations—and Geshem says it is true—that you and the Jews are plotting to revolt, and therefore you are building the wall. Moreover, according to these reports you are about to become their king and have even appointed prophets to make this proclamation about you in Jerusalem: 'There is a king in Judah!' Now this report will get back to the king; so come, let us confer together." (Nehemiah 6:5–7 NIV)

Sanballat's charge was patently false and completely uncorroborated. "Geshem says it is true" is like Al Capone serving as a character witness for Bernie Madoff. Earlier, when Nehemiah was peppered with criticism, he chose to ignore the critics and keep working. However, when Sanballat lobbed the attack ad over the wall, Nehemiah responded:

> I sent him this reply: "Nothing like what you are saying is happening; you are just making it up out of your head." They were all trying to

> frighten us, thinking, "Their hands will get too weak for the work, and
> it will not be completed." But I prayed, "Now strengthen my hands."
> (Nehemiah 6:8–9 NIV)

Although Nehemiah responded, he didn't overreact. His response was twofold: he prayed, and he told the truth. That was the end of it. Sanballat's attack ad was a dud. Why? Because Nehemiah was a man of unquestioned integrity. Nehemiah's credibility as a leader was so unimpeachable that when he said, "It's not true," everyone believed him and went on about their business. In speaking about integrity, CBS's honored and award-winning radio and television journalist Edward R. Murrow said, "To be persuasive we must be believable; to be believable we must be credible; to be credible we must be truthful."[107] More importantly, God said in Proverbs 10:9: "The man of integrity walks securely" (NIV), and in Proverbs 12:19: "Truthful lips will be established forever" (NASB95).

The importance of integrity is emphasized in almost every book on leadership available today, so I'm not going to dwell at length on it here. God set the standard for integrity a long time ago when Moses came off of the mountain and told the people, "don't cheat . . . don't steal . . . don't lie" (my twenty-first century rendition of Exodus 20:14–16). There isn't much I can add to that. Let me be clear and emphatic: *if you do not have integrity, people will not follow you.* If you had it but lost it, they will stop following you. Nehemiah had it, and so must you if you want to lead.

BENEDICT ARNOLD

Benedict Arnold. Judas Iscariot. Marcus Brutus. Speak their names out loud. Does your blood pressure rise? Is anger stirring inside? Few words raise our ire more than "traitor," and there are few things that hurt more than betrayal, especially when the traitor is among our inner circle of close friends and trusted advisors. Once betrayed, life is never the same, as playwright Tennessee Williams said in his play *Camino Real*: "We have to distrust each other. It is our only defense against betrayal."[108]

Benedict Arnold betrayed his country because he was passed over for promotion in the Continental Army, even though he was a favorite of General George Washington. Arnold was a brave and effective general who played a key role in the capture of Fort Ticonderoga in 1775. He fought for the Continentals for four more years, but then turned his back on his country and went over to the British, even fighting for them. Every school-age child knows about Benedict Arnold, and no one wants to play his part in the school play.

Judas betrayed Jesus for thirty pieces of silver. Judas was hand picked by Jesus to be one of the original twelve disciples. He had seen every miracle and heard every sermon. Still, after three years, he betrayed Jesus with a kiss on that fateful night in the garden of Gethsemane: "Judas, are you betraying the Son of Man with a kiss?" (Luke 22:48 NASB95).

Marcus Brutus betrayed Julius Caesar on the infamous "ides of March." He was a close friend of Caesar, the son of his mistress. But that didn't stop him from joining sixty other Roman senators in a conspiracy to assassinate Caesar. You likely remember Shakespeare's version of Caesar's famous dying words, "*Et tu*, Brute?" from your high school literature course.

Back at the wall, Sanballat was running out of ideas. His dirty trick had failed, his attack ads had failed, and he was running out of time. The wall was nearly finished, and the gates would soon be hung in place. He decided he had to play his "ace in the hole"—Shemaiah—his secret informer, an insider well known to Nehemiah:

> One day I went to the house of Shemaiah son of Delaiah, the son of Mehetabel, who was shut in at his home. He said, "Let us meet in the house of God, inside the temple, and let us close the temple doors, because men are coming to kill you—by night they are coming to kill you." But I said, "Should a man like me run away? Or should one like me go into the temple to save his life? I will not go!" I realized that God had not sent him, but that he had prophesied against me because Tobiah and Sanballat had hired him. He had been hired to intimidate me so that I would commit a sin by doing this, and then they would give me a bad name to discredit me. (Nehemiah 6:10-13 NIV)

Nehemiah's courage and integrity thwarted Tobiah and Sanballat's plan and exposed Shemaiah for the traitor he was. "Should a man like me run away?" Nehemiah knew that if he ran from danger, everyone else would too, and the wall project would stall out in the Red Zone. "Should one like me go into the temple to save his life? I will not go!" Nehemiah correctly discerned that Shemaiah was trying to trick him into entering a part of the temple that was forbidden to all but the priests: "I would commit a sin by doing this, and then they would give me a bad name to discredit me."

The potential for betrayal exists in every relationship, in every family, in every organization. Whereas it is not true that "every man has his price," it is true that real or imagined wounds (Benedict Arnold), promises of reward (Judas and Shemaiah), and political jealousy and fear (Brutus) can spur traitorous acts from unexpected sources. There is nothing leaders can do to guarantee they will never be betrayed, but fortunately most leaders will not be blindsided by it in a serious way.

Dirty tricks, attack ads, and possible betrayal are part of the leadership journey. They can come at any time, but especially in the Red Zone. It is common to be sidetracked and stopped by these last-ditch defense efforts and settle for a field goal. It is not common to unwaveringly drive across the goal line. In football, the *elite* quarterbacks do. In wall building . . . or business building . . . or church building . . . *elite* leaders do. Nehemiah did; he would not be stopped by Sanballat's Red Zone attacks, and you won't be either if Leadership Stone #13 is part of your leadership mindset.

Leadership STONE 13 PRESS ON, NO MATTER WHAT.

After criticism from outsiders, threats of *"we will kill them,"* fatigue and infighting between the workers and the rulers, Nehemiah was beset with dirty tricks, attack ads, and betrayal in the ranks. It would have been easy for Nehemiah to throw in the towel, thinking, *What's the use?* The closer he got to the finish line, the harder it was to keep going, but he did keep going. He reminds me of the apostle Paul: "Not that I have already obtained it . . . but I press on toward the goal . . . " (Philippians 3:12–14 NASB95). For Nehemiah, it was, "The wall isn't finished yet, and the opposition hasn't given up yet, but I haven't either. I press on." Pressing on is not easy, but you can and must if you are the leader. Pressing on means:

- Standing courageously and strong. Just before Joshua was to lead the Israelites across the Jordan River into Canaan, God said three times he would need to *"be strong and courageous"* (Joshua 1). Joshua was. Nehemiah was. You will need to be.
- Not compromising your values or God's Word just because things get tough, and it may be expedient to do so. Remember Proverbs 10:9: "The man of integrity walks securely" (NIV).

- Being ever aware and alert so you won't be blindsided. Look for inconsistencies, but don't become paranoid and look for a traitor behind every bush.
- Spending more time with your inner circle. Be especially sensitive to signs of a wounded or disappointed insider.
- Not collapsing into depression when attacked or betrayed. You were not the first, and you won't be the last.
- Not responding in kind. If I remember correctly, God's Word says something about actually loving our enemies, praying for them, blessing them, and even doing good to them (see Luke 6:27–28).
- Pressing on all the way to the finish line. Leadership is hard, especially if you are trying to accomplish something significant. If you are thrown off track by every dirty trick, attack ad, or traitor in the ranks, you will never get the wall finished.

Are you near the goal line, and it seems harder than ever to keep going? Press on!

Are you harassed by dirty tricks and untrue attack ads? Press on!

Has someone close to you gone over to the enemy? Press on!

The goal line is in sight—press on! ●

14

NOTHING UNDONE

The difference between good and great is attention to detail.[109]
Chuck Swindoll

It's been hard to keep people focused these last few days. Once the walls were up, people began to slack off, talking and laughing while sitting on top of the wall. But not Nehemiah. He has been relentless, hollering at everyone that "The job isn't finished yet! The celebration can wait. The gates aren't up, and we need regular schedules for opening and closing them. Guards need to be assigned. Sanballat is still out there and could attack at any moment if we don't finish the job!"

When the sun came up this morning, we had four gates left without doors: the Dung Gate, the Water Gate, the Sheep Gate, and the Old Gate. By mid-afternoon, they were all up except the Sheep Gate. Some of the men suggested it could wait a few days. Of course, Nehemiah would have none of that. He grabbed me, and the two of us tried putting the doors in place by ourselves. They were way too big. Fortunately, when some others saw us struggling, they jumped in to help, and just before sundown we dropped the bolts in place and swung the doors closed. There was a huge cheer all around the city. The wall was finished . . . completely finished. There was nothing undone at all.

Sunday is the big day—we will dedicate the wall and celebrate. Meanwhile, the city has really emptied out. Everyone has gone home to rest, take a bath, prepare the food for the feast, and get their party clothes out of the closet. We'll start solemnly enough, with the priests leading worship and offering sacrifices of thanksgiving. Then the street choirs and parades will ramp things up a bit. We'll cap the day off with music, dancing, and lots of food and drink. There hasn't been an occasion this big in Jerusalem since the temple was completed. They'll probably hear us as far away as Bethany.

And then there's my new job. Nehemiah kept hinting that he had something special in store for me, but I'm a bit humbled (maybe even a little overwhelmed) that he would want me to be his new mayor of Jerusalem. Starting on Monday! I wonder what kind of politician I'll be?

NEHEMIAH'S JOURNAL

"When word came to Sanballat, Tobiah, Geshem the Arab and the rest of our enemies that I had rebuilt the wall and not a gap was left in it—though up to that time I had not set the doors in the gates . . . . " (Nehemiah 6:1 NIV)

"So the wall was completed on the twenty-fifth of Elul, in fifty-two days." (Nehemiah 6:15 NIV)

"After the wall had been rebuilt and I had set the doors in place, the gatekeepers and the singers and the Levites were appointed. I put in charge of Jerusalem my brother Hanani, along with Hananiah the commander of the citadel, because he was a man of integrity and feared God more than most men do. I said to them, 'The gates of Jerusalem are not to be opened until the sun is hot. While the gatekeepers are still on duty, have them shut the doors and bar them. Also appoint residents of Jerusalem as guards, some at their posts and some near their own houses.'" (Nehemiah 7:1–3 NIV)

:: :: :: ::

STOP THE MUSIC

One of my joys in high school was basketball. I was seldom a starter, but as the first man off the bench, I contributed enough to earn a letter.

Our (Chamblee High) big rival was Cross Keys High. We loved to date their girls, but we hated to lose to their guys in *any* sport. They were an easy mark in football, but in basketball they were usually better than we were, so wins were few and far between. My junior year, we got them in our cracker-box gym and played our best game of the year. With one minute and five seconds to go, we had a five-point lead and possession of the ball. We could taste victory, and our jubilant fans, confused by the clock, began a countdown—five . . . four . . . three . . . two . . . one—when actually there was another full minute left in the game. One of our players (unnamed to protect the guilty) threw the ball in the air and began to celebrate. Well, you can guess what happened. They got the ball, scored six points to our zero in the last minute and beat us 66–65.

STOP THE MUSIC. There's a minute left in the game.

Nehemiah's story started when his brother told him the remnant in Jerusalem "who survived the exile . . . are in great trouble and disgrace. The wall of Jerusalem is broken down, and its gates have been burned with fire" (Nehemiah 1:3 NIV). For four months Nehemiah passionately prayed and purposefully planned. Then—against all odds—King Artaxerxes approved Nehemiah's request to go to Jerusalem to rebuild the walls, even appointing him as the new governor of Judah. Nehemiah arrived in Jerusalem and inspired the people to rebuild the wall:

> "You see the trouble we are in: Jerusalem lies in ruins, and its gates have been burned with fire. Come, let us rebuild the wall of Jerusalem, and we will no longer be in disgrace." I also told them about the gracious hand of my God upon me and what the king had said to me. They replied, "Let us start rebuilding." So they began this good work. (Nehemiah 2:17–18 NIV)

In spite of death threats from fierce and determined enemies and dissension and traitors within the ranks, the people "worked with all their heart" (Nehemiah 4:6 NIV). The walls went up and were finished in only fifty-two days. In less than two months, during the hottest part of the year, a 142-year-old pile of rubble was transformed into a mile-and-a-half long wall around the city of Jerusalem. Wow! It was time to have a party. Put on your dancing shoes. Crank up the band. Break out the champagne. Well, it would have been time for all that if Nehemiah wasn't a party pooper. The walls may have been finished, but Nehemiah "had not set the doors in the gates" (Nehemiah 6:1 NIV).

STOP THE MUSIC. We haven't finished the gates yet.

TYING UP LOOSE ENDS

"I have a few loose ends to tie up, and then I'll be home." Does that sound like a familiar phone conversation at the end of a long day? Sometimes those loose ends take a few minutes; sometimes, an hour or more. They can be cleaning out your inbox, returning a phone call or two, or packing up your briefcase for an early morning flight. Whatever the loose ends are, the trip home will rest easy on your mind if they are done. And if they aren't, sleep comes hard that night, because a rope, or business, or church, or life with loose ends has a way of coming unraveled.

For Nehemiah, the wall was finished, but the task wasn't—not completely. So before the party, Nehemiah made sure that all the loose ends were tied off (see Nehemiah 7:1–3 NIV):

- He *set the doors in place.* What good is a wall if the gates have no doors?
- He appointed *the gatekeepers.* What good are gates if there is no one responsible and accountable to open and close them?
- Since he was governor of the whole region of Judah, he needed a mayor (that's what we would call it today) to be *in charge of Jerusalem.* He appointed his *brother, Hanani, along with Hananiah the commander of the citadel* (today's police chief).
- He made sure there were orders in place as to when to open and close the gates: *The gates of Jerusalem are not to be opened until the sun is hot. While the gatekeepers are still on duty, have them shut the doors and bar them.*
- He also appointed *residents of Jerusalem as guards.*

It is common today for leaders to believe that "details" are beneath them—"I leave the details to my staff." Great leaders don't buy into this I-don't-do-details line of thinking. In the business world, no one has ever understood this better than Steve Jobs. From the iMac . . . to the iPod and iTunes . . . to the iPhone . . . and finally to the iPad, Jobs was obsessive about personally ensuring that every detail met the standard of excellence he expected in Apple products. General Colin Powell, who served our country ably as both the chairman of the Joint Chiefs of Staff and as the secretary of state, had this to say about details: "Never neglect details. When everyone's mind is dulled or distracted the leader must be doubly vigilant."[110] *Never neglect details.* Wow! Never? Really? That's what he said—and he's right.

History is full of missed details that brought down nations, companies, individuals, and organizations of all kinds. The Greeks defeated the Trojans because someone forgot to look inside the Trojan Horse. In the late 1990s, a Mars Orbiter satellite was designed partly in metrics and partly in English units. What happened? The navigation system malfunctioned, and the craft was lost in space. In 1994, a safety valve left off of a pipe caused an explosion that killed 167 men on the Piper Bravo oil rig. As the old saying goes, the devil is in the details. I am not saying that the leader has to personally take care of every detail, but the leader does have to be "doubly vigilant" to make sure that every detail is taken care of. Nehemiah did. Steve Jobs did. Colin Powell did. You do, too.

THE FAT LADY CAN SING NOW

Monday Night Football has been around since 1970. Today, it is a slick ESPN production with a fast-paced HD musical entrée, followed by humorless but expert play-by-play announcers and commentators—as serious as if the future of mankind is at stake in the game's outcome. It used to be a lot more fun in the '70s. Howard Cosell was the caustic, self-absorbed, controversial commentator from Brooklyn whom everyone loved to hate but also loved to watch. The counter to Cosell was former Dallas quarterback "Dandy Don" Meredith, a relaxed good ol' cowboy from Mount Vernon, Texas. Meredith didn't take much of anything too seriously. He also provided the musical entertainment that came near the end of the show. As soon as the outcome of the game was certain, Meredith would serenade us with Willie Nelson's "Turn Out the Lights, the Party's Over." If the game was close and the outcome uncertain, Meredith would remind us that "it ain't over 'til the fat lady sings"—his way of saying, "Don't turn off the TV yet."

The "fat lady sings" reference has its roots in opera. Operas often end with an earsplitting blockbuster aria by a mezzo-soprano who is usually a bit large (it takes a lot of lungs to sing opera). Opera goers would say, "The opera isn't over until the fat lady sings." (Unlike Meredith, *they* don't say "ain't".)

One of the responsibilities of leaders is to make sure that the fat lady gets a chance to sing, especially at the successful end of a long hard road—

like building a wall from 142-year-old ruins, moving into a new church building, introducing a revolutionary new product, or the ending of tax season. For some of us that is hard. If you are like me, parties aren't your thing. My normal reaction at the end of a project is, "That's great; what's next?" However, most people aren't like me (a good thing). They need time to celebrate and get a "great job" slap on the back from the leader and their coworkers. They want to reminisce about how hard the job was, to laugh again about the time John fell asleep at his desk or when Jane showed up with her hair going in nine different directions. Celebration provides the emotional closure to a project, necessary before moving on to whatever happens to be the "next big thing."

For Nehemiah, the wall was finished, the gates were hung, Jerusalem had a mayor and chief of police, and 24/7 guards were assigned. There was nothing undone; all the loose ends were tied off. Finally, it was time for the fat lady to sing and the party to begin:

> **At the dedication of the wall of Jerusalem, the Levites were sought out from where they lived and were brought to Jerusalem to celebrate joyfully the dedication with songs of thanksgiving and with the music of cymbals, harps and lyres. (Nehemiah 12:27 NIV)**

Nehemiah called them together and they had "an exuberant celebration because God had filled them with great joy. The women and children raised their happy voices with all the rest. Jerusalem's jubilation was heard far and wide" (Nehemiah 12:43 *The Message*). You can't sing "turn out the lights, the party's over" unless you have a party in the first place. Nehemiah wanted to make sure there was "nothing undone," so they had a party!

Leadership STONE 14 DO SWEAT THE SMALL STUFF.

Richard Carlson made a lot of money with his 1997 book *Don't Sweat the Small Stuff. . . and it's all small stuff.* It was a *USA Today* best seller for two straight years. The book's subtitle is: *Simple Ways to Keep the Little Things from Taking Over Your Life.* The point of the book is to suggest how we can live a more relaxed and satisfying life. The chapter titles reflect the flavor of the book: #13, "Become More Patient" and #18, "Allow Yourself to Be Bored"—good advice for all of us. One of the really relevant chapters for leaders, though, is #16: "Ask Yourself the Question: Will This Matter a Year from Now?" If you are a leader, most everything you do should matter a year from now, and if it doesn't, you probably shouldn't be spending much time on it. If something does matter a year from now, *it's not small stuff,* and somebody needs to sweat about it. Otherwise, the gates are left open at night or a safety valve is left off or a satellite navigation system malfunctions.

David Lloyd George, prime minister of Great Britain during World War I, once said, "There is nothing so fatal to character as half-finished tasks."[111] I disagree. Tasks that are only 99 percent finished can be just as fatal. Ask the families of the men who died on the Piper Bravo oil rig how they felt about a task 99 percent finished. One of the things that makes life and leadership hard is that there is a lot of small stuff to sweat. Nehemiah didn't hang the gates himself, but he made sure it happened. The leader's job is to make sure that the party doesn't start until there is "nothing undone."

Who is responsible for the small stuff in your organization? You are.

Who is responsible to make sure that all the loose ends are tied off? You are.

Who is responsible to make sure the fat lady stays in the Green Room until it's time for her to sing? You are.

And who is responsible to let her out when there is nothing important left undone? You are.

Are you, personally, or your organization at risk because some "detail" is being left undone? If you want to be a Level 5 leader, you should follow Indra Nooyi's (CEO of PepsiCo) example: "I pick up the details that drive the organization insane. But sweating the details is more important than anything else."[112] ▪

15

THE REST OF THE STORY

I have fought the good fight,
I have finished the course.

2 TIMOTHY 4:7 NASB95

How depressing—Nehemiah is leaving next week. I miss him already. In many ways, he's been the heart and soul of Jerusalem for the past twelve years. I can hardly believe it's already been that long since we finished the wall. Didn't we just arrive and start picking up stones? I guess it's no wonder King Artaxerxes is finally asking for Nehemiah to return to Susa. Asking—ha! The "ask" of a king is really a courteous command, so Nehemiah has no choice but to go back. Still, I think, deep down, Jerusalem will remain his "heart home."

I must admit that the last dozen years were amazing. Nehemiah has been a first-rate governor. He always seems to know just what to do. He isn't overbearing. He lets everyone do their job, and when they do well, he always gives them the credit they deserve. He's really made me feel like I've done a good job as the mayor of Jerusalem—which is doubly encouraging because Nehemiah never flatters. He means what he says when he tells someone "well done."

For Nehemiah, it's never about him. It's always about the people and honoring God. I'm still working on that myself, but he is definitely the one I want to emulate—in every way.

When we need help, Nehemiah steps in—sometimes gently, sometimes firmly. He is always fair, and his motive is always to make things right. But one thing for sure: he's especially hard on leaders who take advantage of the people or who violate God's law. He passionately believes Jerusalem is God's chosen city; and the temple, His dwelling place. He moves swiftly and surely when someone does anything that is irreverent and displeasing to God. Of course, he can do it with integrity because he lives what he believes.

It will not be the same here without him. In fact, I wonder what it will take to hold everything together the way we're used to. Nehemiah says he intends to come back, but that's up to the king. Maybe he will; maybe he won't. There's an old saying, "When the cat's away, the mice will play," and that's what worries me. I hope those "mice," Sanballat, Tobiah, Eliashib, and their friends don't try to take over while Nehemiah is gone. If they do, we'll do our best to keep them at bay, but I'll also send word to Nehemiah. He won't want all we've worked for to unravel, and I'm sure he would ask the king for permission to return. Now that is something to look forward to.

NEHEMIAH'S JOURNAL

"Now the city was large and spacious, but there were few people in it, and the houses had not yet been rebuilt. So my God put it into my heart to assemble the nobles, the officials and the common people for registration by families." (Nehemiah 7:4–5 NIV)

"Now the leaders of the people settled in Jerusalem, and the rest of the people cast lots to bring one out of every ten to live in Jerusalem, the holy city, while the remaining nine were to stay in their own towns." (Nehemiah 11:1 NIV)

"Ezra opened the book. All the people could see him because he was standing above them; and as he opened it, the people all stood up. Ezra praised the Lord, the great God; and all the people lifted their hands and responded, 'Amen! Amen!' Then they bowed down and worshiped the Lord with their faces to the ground." (Nehemiah 8:5–6 NIV)

"But while all this was going on, I was not in Jerusalem, for in the thirty-second year of Artaxerxes king of Babylon I had returned to the king. Some time later I asked his permission and came back to Jerusalem. Here I learned about the evil thing Eliashib had done in providing Tobiah a room in the courts of the house of God." (Nehemiah 13:6–7 NIV)

"NOW . . . FOR THE REST OF THE STORY"

"Hello, Americans, I'm Paul Harvey. You know what the news is. In a minute, you're going to hear . . . the *rest* of the story."[113] For more than fifty years, that is how Paul Harvey began his noon radio broadcast to—at its peak—more than 20 million listeners. There is no doubt that if Paul Harvey and Nehemiah had been contemporaries, Nehemiah's story would have been a featured "rest of the story" story.

The rest of Nehemiah's story is told in Nehemiah, chapters 7–13. However, those chapters are less about Nehemiah and more about the people. Nehemiah 7:4–5 documents how the people were registered (today, we would call it a census). Verse 4 tells us that although the walls were rebuilt and the city secure, the "city was large and spacious, but there were few people in it." At Nehemiah's direction, families were designated—by drawing lots—to move into the city so it would be repopulated (Nehemiah 11:1). In Nehemiah 8–10, Ezra the priest takes center stage to lead the people in a time of spiritual renewal: "They bowed down and worshiped the Lord with their faces to the ground." Nehemiah 11 lists the families that resettled in Jerusalem, and Nehemiah 12 lists the priests who served in Jerusalem and Judah.

Chapters 8–12 in Nehemiah are very important in two respects. First, they are a historical record about the Jews and life in the center of their universe, Jerusalem. Second, even more important than their historical value, they bring to the forefront the fact *that God's ultimate purpose is always spiritual*. God's heartbeat is for us to live in a vibrant relationship with Him that brings meaning, direction, and joy to our lives. That is what He wanted for the people of Judah and Jerusalem in Nehemiah's time, and that is what He wants for you and me today. It is not a coincidence that as soon as the wall was finished, the formal dedication of the wall and the party were delayed until after a time of thanksgiving and worship. Nehemiah knew spiritual reformation was God's primary concern, so when the wall was finished, he did something very hard for leaders to do—he stepped out of the spotlight to let Ezra take center stage.

PLAY SECOND FIDDLE

In *Getting Naked*, Patrick Lencioni says, "There is nothing more attractive and admirable than people who willingly and cheerfully set their egos aside and make the needs of others more important than their own."[114] On this point, I love the way Eugene Peterson paraphrases Romans 12:10 in *The Message*. He says there are times when we should "practice playing second fiddle." If you are the "first fiddle" leader, everyone knows. Which means: you don't have to hog the spotlight to make sure they know.

One episode of my leadership experience of which I'm not very proud occurred when an important general was going to visit our facility in Nashville to review the company's progress on a defense project. The visit was arranged by our COO, who was more than qualified to host the visit and knew the general personally. As the CEO, though, I expected to have a role in the program, probably introducing the general to our employees. So the big day arrived, the platform was set up, hundreds of employees gathered, and my role was . . . nothing. I wasn't even part of the plant tour. The COO took care of everything. He introduced the general; he escorted the general on the plant tour; he briefed the general on our project status. And guess what else? The general was pleased and impressed. It was hard for me to accept that it went so well without me. I sulked for days with hurt feelings. I didn't play second fiddle well at all. Jesus warned us about leaders who love the platform: "Beware of the scribes who like . . . respectful greetings in the market places, and chief seats . . . and places of honor at banquets" (Mark 12:38–39 NASB95).

Nehemiah 8 starts with, "All the people gathered together at the square in front of the Water Gate" (HCSB). In addition to the big crowd, there was a high platform. Lots of people . . . and a platform. It was a prime opportunity for Nehemiah to show off a little leadership charisma, garner some applause, and remind the people of all he had done for them. It was the perfect setup for a spotlight-loving leader. However, Nehemiah wasn't a spotlight-loving leader:

Ezra the scribe stood on a high wooden platform built for the occasion. Beside him on his right stood Mattithiah, Shema, Anaiah, Uriah, Hilkiah and Maaseiah; and on his left were Pedaiah, Mishael, Malkijah, Hashum, Hashbaddanah, Zechariah and Meshullam. (Nehemiah 8:4 NIV)

Whose name is missing from this list? *Nehemiah's.* No doubt he was there, but he was probably standing with Hanani in the crowd or possibly off to the side where he could spot any problems that might arise. Maybe he was worried that Sanballat would take advantage of the occasion to launch a surprise attack. Wherever he was, he knew that the people were gathered to "read from the book, from the law of God" (Nehemiah 8:8 NIV), and that was Ezra's job, not his. Nehemiah was the construction foreman and the governor, not the spiritual leader. He wasn't needed on the platform. Unlike me, I suspect he didn't sulk for days because he wasn't the center of attention.

One of a leader's foremost responsibilities is to develop other leaders, and there are several reasons you should stay off the platform at times. First, by stepping aside, you are sending a message that you appreciate and have confidence in the other leaders on your team. It will be a great encouragement to them. Second, how will you know if they can handle the heat of the spotlight if you never let it shine on them? You need to know how they will do when they are in the lead position. Third, by staying off the stage, you let it be known that it is their show and that they deserve the credit and applause. I didn't need to be on the platform when the general visited. It wasn't my show. As hard as it was for me, I *needed* to play second fiddle that day.

PURPOSE LEAKS

Bill Hybels, the senior pastor of Willow Creek Community Church (South Barrington, Illinois), reminds leaders over and over that "vision leaks" if it isn't communicated on a regular basis. I've heard him say it dozens of times, and I have learned that he's right. I've also learned that—especially in large organizations—a lot of things can leak, including *purpose.* Purpose is especially prone to leakage when the leader is complacent or absent. That is why Romans 12:8 insists that we lead with "diligence" (NASB).

Nehemiah had promised King Artaxerxes he would return to Susa after rebuilding the walls: "The king, with the queen sitting beside him, asked, 'How long will you be gone? When will you return?' After I told him how long I would be gone, the king agreed to my request" (Nehemiah 2:6 NLT). "How long" he stayed in Judah before returning to Susa to serve the king turned out to be twelve years (Nehemiah 5:14). However, his heart was always in Jerusalem; so, "Some time later I asked his permission and came back to Jerusalem" (Nehemiah 13:6–7 NIV). When he got back, he found that a significant case of purpose-leak had occurred while he was gone.

During Nehemiah's absence, Eliashib the priest had been given responsibility for the storerooms in the temple. Eliashib was related (by marriage) to Nehemiah's long-standing enemy, Tobiah the Ammonite. Evidently, Tobiah visited Jerusalem frequently, so Eliashib provided him with a convenient place to stay in "a room in the courts of the house of God" (Nehemiah 13:7 NIV). A big deal? Yes. Not only was he an enemy of Nehemiah; more importantly, he was not a Jew and according to the law: "No Ammonite or Moabite or any of his descendants may enter the assembly of the Lord, even down to the tenth generation" (Deuteronomy 23:3 NIV). "No Ammonite" certainly included Tobiah, so when Nehemiah came back, he "was greatly displeased" (Nehemiah 13:8 NIV). A room that was supposed to be used to store "grain offerings and incense and temple articles, and also the tithes of grain, new wine and oil . . . as well as the contributions for the priests" (Nehemiah 13:5 NIV), was being misused as an apartment for *an Ammonite*—a classic example of purpose leak.

Nehemiah didn't waste any time. In order to restore the room to its intended purpose, he did three things (Nehemiah 13:8-9 NIV):

- He "threw all Tobiah's household goods out of the room."
- He "gave orders to purify the rooms."
- He "put back into them the equipment of the house of God, with the grain offerings and the incense."

In other words, he hauled out the trash, swept away the dirt, disinfected the room with industrial-strength cleanser, and brought back what was needed to restore the room to its original purpose. Empty . . . clean . . . fill . . . are simple steps that will work to restore purpose in a lot of situations: your company, your church, your family, your life.

Here is a certain truth: unless the leader is diligent about purpose, it will leak. The purpose at Apple while led by Steve Jobs was to "build an enduring company where people were motivated to build great products. Everything else was secondary . . . products, not the profits, were the motivation".[115] Jobs's replacement will have to be especially diligent to maintain a "products over profit" purpose.

Facebook was started by four Harvard students to provide an easy, cool, and free way for them to connect with their friends. Now that it is a public company with shareholders, will its purpose leak and shareholder value become the driving force?

What about your organization? Has a Tobiah moved in? Do you need an "empty . . . clean . . . fill" day to restore purpose? If you are the leader, it's your job to make that happen.

Leadership STONE 15 KNOW WHEN TO STEP ASIDE; KNOW WHEN TO STEP IN.

It has been many pages since I suggested in the introduction that Nehemiah was a Level 5 leader according to the criteria established by Jim Collins in *Good to Great*. As I pointed out, Collins identifies Level 5 leaders as having first, "personal humility" and second, "fierce resolve." They are willing to step aside and play second fiddle when they need to, letting others have the stage and spotlight. They do not seek celebrity status, and they don't have CEO Disease.

However, when they need to step in, they do so with fierce resolve. They don't shrink back or hesitate, especially when purpose, values, or vision are at risk. The best example of this in the Bible is when Jesus stepped in because the temple was not being used for its intended purpose:

> He found the Temple teeming with people selling cattle and sheep and doves. The loan sharks were also there in full strength. Jesus put together a whip out of strips of leather and chased them out of the Temple, stampeding the sheep and cattle, upending the tables of the loan sharks, spilling coins left and right. He told the dove merchants, "Get your things out of here! Stop turning my Father's house into a shopping mall!" (John 2:14–16 *The Message*)

A whip . . . stampede . . . overturned tables . . . "Get out of here" . . . that sounds like fierce resolve to me.

Are you willing to play second fiddle and let others take the lead and stand in the spotlight at times?

Are you willing to step in and restore leaking purpose in your organization—or in your life?

Are you making progress toward Level 5?

You can, if you follow Nehemiah's example. ■

16

CAN YOU LEAD LIKE NEHEMIAH?

May the favor of the Lord our God rest upon *you*;
establish the work of *your* hands . . .
yes, establish the work of *your* hands.

(PSALM 90:17 PERSONALIZED BY AUTHOR)

When Nehemiah returned, it felt like the whole city of Jerusalem breathed a sigh of relief. To say the least, things had slipped a bit while he was gone. And like with the original wall project, Nehemiah didn't waste any time setting things right. He cleaned Tobiah out of the temple, insisted that the people bring grain, wine, and oil as provisions for the temple and priests, and he shut down all trading and working on the Sabbath. It's good to again have a governor who fears God and obeys His commands.

Nehemiah hit the ground running when he first arrived, but lately he's been quiet and fairly contemplative. He's spent a lot of time writing the story of rebuilding the walls. It's almost as if he knows his time in the spotlight will be over soon and wants to make sure his legacy honors and pleases God. He doesn't care too much what people say about him; he cares a lot about what God will say when his turn comes to stand before Him. Personally, I don't think he has a thing to worry about. He's been an exceptional leader—always leading with great faith and with great confidence in God.

Ironic. They said it couldn't be done—rebuilding the wall. But Nehemiah and God did it. Actually, Nehemiah says it was only because of God's gracious hand that he was able to accomplish anything meaningful at all. Everyone wonders who will replace Nehemiah someday. It's hard to imagine anyone filling his shoes. Will it be someone who leads like he does? We can only hope so.

NEHEMIAH'S JOURNAL

"Remember me for this, O my God, and do not blot out what I have so faithfully done for the house of my God and its services." (Nehemiah 13:14 NIV)

"Remember me for this also, O my God, and show mercy to me according to your great love." (Nehemiah 13:22 NIV)

"Remember me with favor, O my God." (Nehemiah 13:31 NIV)

⸝⸝   ⸝⸝   ⸝⸝   ⸝⸝

NEHEMIAH'S RÉSUMÉ

When a new leader arrives at a business or church or state agency, the halls are often lined with cynics and skeptics who have a lot of spoken—and unspoken—questions and doubts: *Who is this guy? What makes her think she can save this business? The last three CEOs failed. Our church has been in decline for ten years. What makes him think he can make a difference? Our products are "old school," and our factories are run-down, low-tech. How can a new general manager overcome that?* The new leader often tries to win them over by parading out his credentials and track record of success: MBA from an Ivy League university, led turnarounds at three companies, PhD in theology, first female CEO of a Fortune 100 company, started a church that grew to 10,000 in only five years, and so on, and so forth, and so what.

When Nehemiah showed up in Jerusalem to lead the wall building project, he undoubtedly faced a skeptical audience of Jews with a lot of spoken—and unspoken—questions and doubts: *Who is this guy? What makes him think this wall can be rebuilt? Doesn't he know that Sanballat and his allies will do everything in their power to stop him? Isn't he just another one of the king's lackeys?*

Nehemiah didn't win them over with his credentials (the king's cupbearer and now governor of Judah), and he couldn't boast about his track record of successful wall-building projects (there weren't any). He had a one-entry résumé: "I told them how the gracious hand of my God had been on me" (Nehemiah 2:18 HCSB). The king had sent him—that much was good. His brother Hanani was well known—that was good, too. He had considerable power because he was the governor—good again. But what really carried the day was "the gracious hand of God" on him. So the people responded with, "Let's start rebuilding" (Nehemiah 2:18 HCSB).

The title of this chapter is a question: "Can You Lead Like Nehemiah?" I don't know what you face as a leader. I do know that whatever is in front of you, you have two ways of trying to get it done. You can go it alone, or you can lead like Nehemiah with the gracious hand of God on you. I won't insult you by suggesting you cannot achieve success in this world without the hand of God on you; you can. However, if you do, so what? After the retirement party and your last interview on CNBC, what then? If you are mega-successful, you may get a short article in the *Wall Street Journal* when you die. You may be able to lead your organization without God's hand on you, but why would you want to, and what is the point? One of the most successful leaders of all time found out the hard way that there is no point in dying as . . .

THE RICHEST MAN IN THE CEMETERY[116]

About 500 years before the story of Nehemiah, Solomon succeeded David as the king of Israel and reigned for 40 years in Jerusalem. He got off to a great start, loving God and walking in obedience to God's law (1 Kings 3:3). He asked God for wisdom, and men came from all over the world "to hear the wisdom of Solomon" (1 Kings 4:34 NASB). He was the most powerful man of his time—and the wealthiest. Solomon's kingdom enjoyed both peace and prosperity during his reign. He was on a roll until he contracted CEO Disease. That's when it became *all about him.*

Somewhere along the way, Solomon forgot about God and forgot about the people he was supposed to be leading. He sought after his own pleasure, expanded his businesses, built more and bigger houses, and accumulated so much wealth that today he would be #1 on the *Forbes* list. He "became great and increased more than all who preceded" him (Ecclesiastes 2:9 NASB). He "did not refuse . . . did not withhold" (Ecclesiastes 2:10 NASB) anything his eyes or heart desired. He was spectacularly successful by the standards of his day—for that matter, by the standards of *any* day. However, near the end of his life when the young lions were posturing to take his place, when there was no more wealth to gain and no more awards to win, and when women had quit swooning when he walked into the room, he summed up his life this way: "As I looked at everything I had worked so hard to accomplish, it was all so meaningless—like chasing the wind. There was nothing really worthwhile anywhere" (Ecclesiastes 2:11 NLT).

Solomon's publicist would have written an obituary that needed two full pages in the *Jerusalem Gazette,* but even though he died the richest man in the cemetery and the one "with the most toys," if Solomon had written his own version of his obituary, it would have been short and sad (dates approximate):

Solomon, son of David

Born: 1000 BC

Died: 930 BC

A meaningless life that accomplished

nothing really worthwhile at all.

Did Solomon's life have to be meaningless? No, and he concludes his story by telling us that if he could do it all over again he would: "Fear God and obey his commands, for this is everyone's duty" (Ecclesiastes 12:13–14 NLT).

Nehemiah must have read Solomon's conclusion and taken it to heart. "Fear God and obey his commands" is how he lived and how he led. "Obey his commands" is easy for us to understand, yet hard to do. But "fear God": what does that mean?

For sure, it doesn't mean to be *afraid* of God. Bible scholars use words like "respect" or "honor" or "have reverence for" to explain "fear God." To me, it means to *take Him seriously*. Take seriously who He is—the Creator and Sustainer of all life. Take seriously what He says in His written word, the Bible. Take seriously that He wants us to love Him and have a personal relationship with Him like Nehemiah did. Take seriously that He wants to be involved in all aspects of our lives, not just on Sunday, but Monday through Friday at the office and on Saturday at the golf course or the mall. Take seriously that we will all someday have to stand before Him to give an account of our life. Solomon knew he would have to: "God will judge us for everything we do, including every secret thing, whether good or bad" (Ecclesiastes 12:14 NLT).

Nehemiah took God seriously. He did fear God and obey His commands. He was ready to stand before God and give an account of his life. If we do the same, our résumé can look like Nehemiah's: "the gracious hand of my God had been on me." That's a lot better than an MBA from . . . well, anywhere.

BUT THAT WAS THEN

This is the twenty-first century. Life is different than it was in Nehemiah's time. All he had to deal with were a few farmers, some shopkeepers, and enemies who were nothing more than poorly trained militia. He may have needed God, but I don't see the relevance of God to my life today, especially at work. Nehemiah didn't have to cope with a global economy in a lightning-fast digital world. He didn't have to face a bunch of Wall Street analysts with profit reports every month. He didn't have to compete with low-cost Chinese labor. And he didn't have to wade through five levels of bureaucracy to get a building permit.

All true.

Nehemiah didn't face the same modern challenges you face. However, Norm Miller, Truett Cathy, Anthony Rossi, Joe Gibbs, Mary Kay Ash, and Henry Parsons Crowell all did (Miller, Cathy, and Gibbs still do).

Norm Miller is the Chairman of Interstate Batteries, a $1+ billion corporation with 1,400 employees. Interstate is the #1 replacement battery in America today, with more than 200,000 retail distributors. They know all about low-cost competition in a global economy. Do they take God seriously? Yes. As highlighted on their website, their mission is:

> To glorify God as we supply our customers worldwide with top quality, value-priced batteries, related electrical power-source products, and distribution services. Further, our mission is to provide our partners and team members with opportunities which are profitable, rewarding and growth-oriented.[117]

Chick-fil-A is led by founder and chairman Truett Cathy and his sons, Dan and Donald. It is the second largest quick-service chicken restaurant chain in the United States, with more than 1,500 locations and annual sales exceeding $4 billion. Does the Cathy family take God seriously? According to Truett Cathy, the family operates with a "business philosophy based on biblical principles,"[118] and its corporate purpose is "To glorify God by being faithful stewards of all that is entrusted to us."[119]

Anthony Rossi founded Tropicana Products, the company that produces the Tropicana orange juice you can find in most any grocery store or gas station. Rossi led Tropicana for more than thirty years, building it into the leading citrus juice producer in the US. Did he take God seriously? Yes. So much so that his Christian faith is featured in the title of his biography: *Anthony T. Rossi, Christian and Entrepreneur: The Story of the Founder of Tropicana*. The book description on Amazon says this about Rossi: "He also found a vibrant faith in God that touched his business and personal dealings daily."[120]

Joe Gibbs, the winning coach of three Super Bowls and owner of three NASCAR championship teams, is a successful leader who takes God seriously. In a 2011 interview with Sally Quinn of the *Washington Post*, Gibbs said, "We have the greatest head coach of all—God," and in the Bible, we have "the ultimate playbook."[121] The "greatest head coach . . . the ultimate playbook"—that is taking God very seriously.

Henry Parsons Crowell, the founder of Quaker Oats, was another successful leader who took God seriously. His story as recounted on wikipedia says, "Crowell viewed all things as a stewardship from God," and "In whatever he did, Crowell sought to honor God."[122]

Mary Kay Cosmetics (more than $2 billion in annual sales) is named for its founder, Mary Kay Ash. She led Mary Kay for thirty years, taking God seriously the whole time. The company was "founded not on the competitive rule, but on the Golden Rule, on praising people to success and on the principle of placing faith first, family second and career third."[123]

Batteries, chicken sandwiches, orange juice, football, stock car racing, cereal, and cosmetics—all led by successful, winning leaders who took God seriously. They were, and are, Nehemiah-type leaders with the *gracious hand of God* on them. Although their businesses are strikingly different, they all have one crucial thing in common: the same starting point.

THE STARTING POINT

The starting point for God's gracious hand on you is *not* going to church. It is not reading the Bible. It is not promising God that you will obey the Ten Commandments if He blesses you. The starting point for leading like Nehemiah is having a personal and vibrant relationship with God through faith in His Son, Jesus Christ: "So now we can rejoice in our wonderful new relationship with God because our Lord Jesus Christ has made us friends of God" (Romans 5:11 NLT). This verse says clearly that we can have a relationship with God, but not because we are good or successful or give a lot of money to charity or are born into the right family or church. Relationship with God is *because of our Lord Jesus Christ.*

I realize that some of you may be thinking: *Oh no, not that Jesus thing again. Those people from Westboro Baptist Church claim to be followers of Jesus, yet they are out demonstrating at the funerals of soldiers. And every time I turn on the news there is some story about a priest or pastor molesting a child or some televangelist ripping off widows by taking their Social Security money so he can fly around in his private jet. If that is what it means to have a relationship with Jesus, it's not for me. I sure don't want to be identified with any of them.*

I don't blame you, and I don't want to be identified with any of them either. But I didn't abandon the business world and give up my CEO title just because Ken Lay (Enron) and Dennis Kozlowski (Tyco) turned out to be crooks who cast a shadow over all business leaders. Most every barrel has a few rotten apples. That is true in the business barrel and in the church, athletic, government, education, and media/entertainment barrels. In spite of that, I still love to watch the Cowboys beat the Redskins; I still vote; I still watch a movie every now and then. Rotten apples are no reason to throw the whole barrel away. So don't use that as an excuse to not take God seriously and to ignore His Son, Jesus.

I am not going to insult you by suggesting that I can write a paragraph or two, include a prayer for you to say, and without further ado you will fully place your faith in Christ and begin to take God seriously. It is too important a decision for that. What I am suggesting—even begging—is for you to take this matter seriously and commit to do some follow-up reading and contemplation.

You can read Norm Miller's full story in his book *Beyond the Norm* or at www.normanmillerstory.com. You will read that he reached all his goals "ahead of time," but wondered, "Where's the payoff? Is this all there is to life?" He sounds a lot like Solomon, doesn't he?

The story of Truett Cathy's business success is chronicled in *It's Easier to Succeed than to Fail.* Amazon's book summary describes it this way: "Is this a book on business success? Yes. Is this a book on allowing your devotion to

God to affect your dealings in business? Yes. Is this a book about a person's personal walk with God? Yes."[124]

Joe Gibb's book, *Game Plan for Life*, and the biography of Henry Parsons Crowell, *Cereal Tycoon* (by Joe Musser), both tell the story of successful leaders who had the gracious hand of God on them because of their faith in Christ.

Read their stories, and you will discover that a relationship with God is just as relevant for us today as it was for Nehemiah. However, more important than what all these men say is . . . what does the Bible say? It doesn't matter that Joe Gibbs believes or that I believe—a relationship with God comes only through faith in Jesus Christ. However, it does matter *why* we believe it. We believe it because the Bible says it is true:

> Jesus told him, "I am the way, the truth, and the life. No one comes to the Father except through Me. If you know Me, you will also know My Father." (John 14:6–7 HCSB)

> For Jesus is the one referred to in the Scriptures, where it says . . . "There is salvation in no one else! God has given no other name under heaven by which we must be saved." (Acts 4:11–12 NLT)

You don't have to take seriously what I say. You don't even have to take Joe Gibbs or Truett Cathy seriously. But if the Bible says, "No one comes to the Father except through me" and "There is salvation in no one else," I suggest you consider those words seriously. In spite of the popular notion that there are many paths to God, the Bible says there is only one path—faith in Jesus Christ. Don't get upset with me; God is the One who says that. If you want to argue, argue with Him.

Still not convinced? Neither was Lee Strobel. After graduating from the University of Missouri (journalism) and Yale (law), Strobel was an award-winning journalist for fourteen years, including a stint as the legal editor of *The Chicago Tribune*. When his agnostic wife became a Christian, Strobel decided to use his journalism and legal training to intensively investigate the validity of Christianity, especially the claims of Christ. When Strobel started, "I was a skeptic. In fact, I considered myself an atheist."[125] When he was finished, he concluded that it takes more faith to *not* believe than to believe. His first two books, *The Case for Faith* and *The Case for Christ*, are worth your time if you are a skeptic, or even an atheist, but are curious about what Strobel learned that convinced him to take God seriously.

IT'S NOT COMPLICATED

The most familiar verse in the Bible is "For God loved the world in this way: He gave His One and Only Son, so that everyone who believes in Him will not perish but have eternal life" (John 3:16 HCSB). You see this verse everywhere—on billboards, t-shirts, on signs at football games, tattooed on the forearms of 300-pound offensive linemen, and stitched on the hats of professional bull rider cowboys. The first two Bible verses I learned as a child were 1 John 4:16, "God is love," and John 3:16. If asked, millions of people would say they are Christ followers because of the truth of John 3:16.

Have you wondered what John 3:16 really means and if its message is for you, too? Rather than trying to convince you here, if you really want to know, would you be willing to invest forty-five minutes in a clear and simple explanation of John 3:16? It is a sermon by Andy Stanley, pastor of North Point Community Church in Alpharetta, Georgia (a northern suburb of Atlanta). The premise of Stanley's message is that John 3:16 is good news for everyone, and it is not complicated. If you are at all interested in taking God seriously and having a relationship with Him, please take time to watch it at www.yourmove.is/watch/uncomplicating-christmas. I think you may be surprised to learn that knowing God really is not complicated, and it really is good news.

THE ANSWER IS . . . YES

The story of Nehemiah is one for the ages. Five hundred years from now . . . one thousand years from now . . . people will still be reading his story and saying, "Wow, he was a true Level 5 leader with God's hand on him!" Leading like Nehemiah means leading with passion, but also being patient. It means being both humble and resolute. It means having vision and the courage to go after it. It means understanding that it's "not about you" and avoiding CEO Disease. It means being thick-skinned and staying focused on purpose—not being distracted by opposition or dissension. It means leaving nothing undone and scoring touchdowns, not field goals. It means knowing when to step aside and when to step in. Nehemiah's story is about the big picture, details, people, enemies, critics, and traitors. The setting of the story is almost 2,500 years ago, but it still resonates for leaders today trying to turn around a company, build a church, or save a government.

Here's the rub. To lead like Nehemiah, it takes more than being a Level 5 leader—it takes God. No matter how good Nehemiah was in his own right, without God's favor, the wall-building project would never have gotten off the ground. The odds were stacked too high against him.

Can you lead like Nehemiah? The answer is, "Yes, you can," but only if you follow his example.

What did we learn from watching him rebuild the walls? We learned he had a personal relationship with God. So can you. We learned he did everything he could do, but depended on God to do what he couldn't. So can you. We learned he was obedient to God's Word, leading in a way that pleased God. So can you. And we learned he had confidence in God. He trusted God fully to bring him success. When he told the people, "Our God will fight for us" (Nehemiah 4:20 NIV), he actually believed it. So can you.

An MBA will teach you a lot about leadership. Experience and mentors can teach you a lot about leadership. You can raise the level of your leadership by attending workshops and reading (see the recommended list in appendix 2). And hopefully, this book is going to help you become a better leader. However, don't miss this: to lead like Nehemiah, you must have a relationship with God, depend on Him, obey Him, and have confidence that He will put His gracious hand on you when you do these things.

Isn't that much better than going it alone?

Leadership STONE 16 BEGIN TODAY TO WRITE YOUR OBITUARY BY HOW YOU LIVE AND LEAD.

At the close of Nehemiah's story, three times he asks God to remember him:

> Remember me for this, O my God, and do not blot out what I have so faithfully done for the house of my God and its services. (Nehemiah 13:14 NIV)

> Remember me for this also, O my God, and show mercy to me according to your great love. (Nehemiah 13:22 NIV)

> Remember me with favor, O my God. (Nehemiah 13:31 NIV)

God remembered. He did not blot out Nehemiah's story. He inscribed it forever in His book, the Bible. God remembers Nehemiah with great favor. All of us who aspire to leadership will do well to remember his story as well.

What will people remember about you? Will you end up like Solomon, wondering if you really accomplished anything worthwhile and lasting? If you are on the same track he was, the words of Jesus should spur some sober thinking on your part: "And what do you benefit if you gain the whole world but lose your own soul? Is anything worth more than your soul?" (Matthew 16:26 NLT).

The good news is that it is not too late to change what people and God remember by living and leading like Nehemiah. My prayer for you is (Psalm 90:17, my paraphrase):

> Let the favor of the Lord our God rest upon you and establish the work of your hands.

APPENDIX 1:

HISTORY OF JERUSALEM

3000–5000 BC

Gihon Springs

Water from the Gihon Spring first attracted settlers to what we now call Jerusalem. The spring was located in the Kidron Valley on the east side of the mountain (elevation: 2,400 feet) that would later be called Mount Moriah ("Solomon began to build the temple of the LORD in Jerusalem on Mount Moriah"—2 Chronicles 3:1 NIV) and today is called the Temple Mount. Little is known about who the first settlers were or where they came from. In ancient documents, the settlement is variously referred to as Rusalimun, Roshlamen, or Urusalim.

2000 BC

Salem (Genesis 14)

The first biblical reference to Jerusalem (Salem) occurs in Genesis 14 when the King of *Salem*, Melchizedek—also a priest of God Most High—served bread and wine to Abram as he was returning from a victorious battle against four kings who had captured his nephew, Lot. Some scholars question whether Salem and Jerusalem are the same site, but Psalm 76:1–2 (NIV) settles it for me: "In Judah God is known; his name is great in Israel. His tent is in Salem, his dwelling place in Zion."

1400 BC

Joshua (Joshua 10)

The city is called Jerusalem in the Bible for the first time in Joshua 10. Adoni-zedek, the king of Jerusalem, was killed in battle as the Israelites invaded and conquered the Promised Land of Canaan. Joshua did not destroy the city, and it continued to be the home of the Jebusites for 400 years thereafter: "Now as for the Jebusites, the inhabitants of Jerusalem, the sons of Judah could not drive them out; so the Jebusites live with the sons of Judah at Jerusalem until this day" (Joshua 15:63 NASB95).

1050 BC

Saul (1 Samuel 9–31)

For three centuries the Israelites lived in Canaan without a king to rule over them. Leaders such as Samson and Gideon (see the book of Judges in the Bible) rose up to lead their armies against their enemies (the Philistines), but the people wanted a king: "Give us a king to judge us like all the other nations have" (1 Samuel 8:5 NLT). So Saul was chosen as the first king of Israel. He reigned for forty years from Gibeah, northwest of Jerusalem (which was still under control of the Jebusites). The only reference to Jerusalem during Saul's reign was after David killed Goliath: "Then David took the Philistine's head and brought it to Jerusalem" (1 Samuel 17:54 NASB95).

1010 BC

David (2 Samuel; 1 Chronicles)

The Philistines routed the Israelites in a battle at Mount Gilboa (1 Samuel 31) where Saul, badly wounded, fell on his own sword rather than fall into the hands of his enemies. David was chosen to replace Saul, initially as the king of Judah: "Then the men of Judah came and there anointed David king over the house of Judah" (2 Samuel 2:4 NASB95). The one remaining son of Saul, Ish-Bosheth, was made king over the northern tribes, but "after a long war between the house of Saul and the house of David" (2 Samuel 3:1), David prevailed and in 1003 BC was anointed king of all Israel. Soon afterward, he captured Jerusalem (2 Samuel 5) and made it the permanent capital of Israel. David reigned for forty years.

970 BC

Solomon (1 Kings 1–11; 2 Chronicles 1–9)

Solomon, David's son by Bathsheba, succeeded David as king of Israel and reigned from Jerusalem for forty years. He was chosen by God to build the first temple (1 Kings 5–8), completing and dedicating it in 960 BC: "The LORD said . . . 'I have consecrated this temple . . . by putting my Name there forever. My eyes and my heart will always be there'" (1 Kings 9:3 NIV). Solomon's temple served as the center of Jewish religious life for almost 400 years.

930 BC

Judah and Israel (1 Kings 12–22; 2 Kings; 2 Chronicles 10–36)

After Solomon's death, a civil war broke out that permanently divided Israel into the Southern Kingdom of Judah and the Northern Kingdom of Israel. Israel was ruled by a succession of nineteen kings, all of whom succumbed to idol worship. They lost God's favor and protection and were conquered by the Assyrians in about 723 BC (2 Kings 17). Jerusalem continued as the capital of Judah (the Southern Kingdom), and Solomon's temple continued as their center of worship. Judah was led by a succession of twenty kings, some of whom were faithful to worship God and received His favor and protection. Judah survived for 137 years longer than Israel. However, reversion to idol worship brought God's judgment, and in 587 BC, King Nebuchadnezzar of Babylon ordered the destruction of Jerusalem and the temple (2 Kings 25; 2 Chronicles 36). Many of the people of Judah were taken into exile to Babylon: "He carried into exile all Jerusalem: all the officers and fighting men, and all the craftsmen and artisans—a total of ten thousand. Only the poorest people of the land were left" (2 Kings 24:14 NIV). It is likely, but not certain, that Nehemiah's grandparents were among those taken from Jerusalem to Babylon and that Nehemiah was born to parents in exile.

538 BC

Return of Jews to Jerusalem (Ezra)

In 539 BC, the Babylonians were conquered by the Persians, led by King Cyrus. One of Cyrus's first acts was to authorize the return of some of the Jews to Jerusalem to rebuild the temple:

> Thus says Cyrus king of Persia, "The LORD, the God of heaven, has given me all the kingdoms of the earth and He has appointed me to build Him a house in Jerusalem, which is in Judah. Whoever there is among you of all His people, may his God be with him! Let him go up to Jerusalem which is in Judah and rebuild the house of the LORD, the God of Israel; He is the God who is in Jerusalem." (Ezra 1:2-3 NASB95)

Led by Zerubbabel, almost 50,000 Jews returned to the vicinity of Jerusalem. Work began on the temple in 536 BC and continued—with several pauses—for about twenty years. It was dedicated in 515 BC:

> This temple was completed on the third day of the month Adar; it was the sixth year of the reign of King Darius. And the sons of Israel, the priests, the Levites and the rest of the exiles, celebrated the dedication of this house of God with joy. (Ezra 6:15–16 NASB95)

For another seventy years, the Jews lived in and around a wall-less Jerusalem, surrounded by enemies. That is when:

> Hanani, one of my brothers, had just arrived from Judah with some fellow Jews. I asked them about the conditions among the Jews there who had survived the exile, and about Jerusalem. They told me, "The exile survivors who are left there in the province are in bad shape. Conditions are appalling. The wall of Jerusalem is still rubble; the city gates are still cinders." When I heard this, I sat down and wept. I mourned for days, fasting and praying before the God-of-Heaven. (Nehemiah 1:2–4 *The Message*)

So it was, in 445 BC, that the story of Nehemiah began.

[Author's Note: These dates in the history of Jerusalem are not universally agreed upon. In your own reading, you will probably run across some that are slightly different from those used above.]

APPENDIX 2:
SUGGESTED READING

Ten personal favorites:

Abraham Lincoln by Ronald C. White Jr.

Courageous Leadership by Bill Hybels

Execution by Larry Bossidy and Ram Charan

How the Mighty Fall by Jim Collins

Leadership Is an Art by Max De Pree

Leadership Jazz by Max De Pree

Proverbs in the Bible

The Progress Principle by Teresa Amabile and Steven Kramer

True North by Bill George

Who Says Elephants Can't Dance? by Louis Gerstner Jr.

Other suggested reading:

Built to Last by Jim Collins and Jerry Porras

The Case for Christ by Lee Strobel

The Case for Faith by Lee Strobel

The Contrarian's Guide to Leadership by Steven B. Sample

Drive by Daniel H. Pink

Eat Mor Chikin by S. Truett Cathy

Endurance by Caroline Alexander

Failing Forward by John Maxwell

First, Break All the Rules by Marcus Buckingham and Curt Coffman

The Five Dysfunctions of a Team by Patrick Lencioni

Getting Naked by Patrick Lencioni

Good to Great by Jim Collins

Great by Choice by Jim Collins and Martin T. Hansen

The Leadership Challenge by James Kouzes and Barry Posner

Leading Change by John P. Kotter

Made to Stick by Chip Heath and Dan Heath

The Servant by James C. Hunter

Steve Jobs by Walter Isaacson

Too Busy Not to Pray by Bill Hybels

The 21 Irrefutable Laws of Leadership by John Maxwell

Unbroken by Laura Hillenbrand

Visioneering by Andy Stanley

Wild Goose Chase by Mark Batterson

ENDNOTES

1   Jim Collins, *Good to Great* (New York: Harper Business, 2001), 22.

2   Ibid., 18.

3   Jim Collins, "The Ten Greatest CEOs of All Time," *Fortune*, July 23, 2003.

4   Ibid.

5   2012 The Global Leadership Summit, August 9–10, 2012, live broadcast from Willow Creek Community Church, South Barrington, IL.

6   Avraham Holtz, *The Holy City: Jews on Jerusalem* (New York: W. W. Norton and Company, Inc., 1971), 11.

7   Lisa Katz, "Jews and Jerusalem: The Source of the Bond," posted at: http://judaism.about.com/od/jerusalem/a/jerslm_jews.htm.

8   Benjamin Disraeli, 1804–1891: British politician, prime minister in 1868 and 1874–1880; quote attributed. Author's note: "quote attributed" means the quote is commonly and widely used, often in dozens of places (websites, blogs, etc.), but the original source is not identified.

9   Field Marshal Ferdinand Foch, 1851–1929: supreme commander of the Allied armies in World War I; quote attributed.

10 E. M. Forster, cited in Gary Hamel, *The Future of Management*, Gary Hamel (Boston: Harvard Business Review Press, 2007), ebook.

11 John Maxwell, *The 21 Indispensable Qualities of a Leader* (Nashville: Thomas Nelson, 1999), 148.

[12]   Jim Collins and Jerry Porras, *Built to Last* (New York: Harper Business, 1994), 54.

[13]   George Merck, cited in Michael Useem, *The Leadership Moment* (New York: Times Business, 1998), 29.

[14]   Posted at: www.TOMS.com.

[15]   James M. Kouzes and Barry Z. Posner, *The Leadership Challenge* (San Francisco: Jossey-Bass, 2002), 185.

[16]   Ibid., 187.

[17]   James C. Hunter, *The Servant* (New York: Crown Business, 1998), 91.

[18]   Albert Einstein, 1879–1955, 1921: Nobel Prize for Physics; quote attributed.

[19]   Patrick Lencioni, *Getting Naked* (San Francisco, Josey-Bass, 2010), 200.

[20]   Louis V. Gerstner Jr., *Who Says Elephants Can't Dance?* (New York: Harper Collins, 2002), 3.

[21]   Maxwell, 85.

[22]   Titus Livius, 59BC–17AD; Roman historian, author of *The History Of Rome*, written in approximately 20-25 BC; quote attributed.

[23]   Arthur Henderson, 1863–1935: British politician and Nobel Peace Prize Laureate; quote attributed.

[24]   Malcolm Gladwell, 1963–: American author of *Tipping Point, Blink, Outliers*, etc.; quote attributed.

[25]   Fred Smith, cited in John Maxwell, *Failing Forward* (Nashville: Thomas Nelson, 2000), 67.

[26]   Andy Stanley, *Visioneering* (Colorado Springs: Multnomah Publishers, 1999), 58.

[27]   Stephen Covey, *The 7 Habits of Highly Effective People* (New York: Simon and Schuster, 1989), 237.

28 George Burns, 1896–1996: American comedian and TV personality; quote attributed.

29 Larry Bossidy and Ram Charan, *Execution* (New York: Crown Business, 2002), 19.

30 Euripides, 480–406 BC, ancient Greek playwright; quote is from *Heracleidae*, written approximately 428 BC.

31 Winston Churchill, 1874–1965: British politician and prime minister during World War II; quote attributed.

32 Bossidy and Charan, 1.

33 Ibid., 6.

34 Lawrence Peter "Yogi" Berra, 1925–: Hall of Fame catcher for the New York Yankees from 1946–1963; quote attributed.

35 General Dwight D. Eisenhower, 1890–1969: five-star general and supreme commander of Allied Forces in Europe, thirty-fourth president of the US; quote attributed.

36 The phrase "don't waste the wait" was given to me by Diane Cobb as part of the content editor review phase of this book.

37 Lencioni, viii.

38 Robert B. Hughes and J. Carl Laney, *Tyndale Concise Bible Commentary* (Wheaton: Tyndale House Publishers, 1990), ebook.

39 Viktor E. Frankl, 1905–1997: Austrian neurologist, psychiatrist, and Holocaust survivor; quote attributed.

40 The 1939 film *The Wizard of Oz* is based on the book by L. Frank Baum, *The Wonderful Wizard of Oz*, originally published in 1900.

41 Thomas A. Edison, 1847–1931: America's most famous inventor with more than 1,000 patents; quote attributed.

42 Bill George, *True North* (San Francisco: John Wiley & Sons, 2007), xxxiii.

[43] Bill Hybels, *Courageous Leadership* (Grand Rapids: Zondervan, 2002), 40.

[44] Ibid., 243.

[45] Ibid., 245.

[46] Ibid., 235.

[47] George, xxxiii.

[48] Hybels, 243.

[49] Laura Hillenbrand, *Unbroken* (New York: Random House, 2010), 366.

[50] Disraeli, quote attributed.

[51] Gerstner, 54.

[52] Lisa Vollmer, "Mulcahy Took a No-Nonsense Approach to Turn Xerox Around," *Stanford Graduate School of Business News*, December 1, 2004.

[53] Max De Pree, *Leadership Is an Art* (New York: Dell Publishing, 1989), 11.

[54] Berra; quote attributed.

[55] Collins and Porras, 91.

[56] Stanley, 8.

[57] Hybels, 29.

[58] Warren G. Bennis and Robert Townsend, *Reinventing Leadership: Strategies to Empower the Organization* (New York: Harper Business, 2005).

[59] Kouzes and Posner, 118.

[60] Lewis Carroll, *Through the Looking Glass* (public domain, 1871).

[61] John P. Kotter, *Leading Change* (Boston: Harvard Business School Press, 1996), 92.

62 John Maxwell, *The 21 Irrefutable Laws of Leadership* (Nashville: Thomas Nelson, 1998), 146.

63 Bossidy and Charan, 19.

64 Ibid., 1.

65 Warren Bennis, 1925–: American author of more than thirty leadership books, professor at leading business schools, dubbed by *Forbes* magazine as the dean of leadership gurus; quote attributed.

66 Maxwell, 146.

67 Ibid., 149.

68 Wikipedia, Shackleton.

69 Warren Bennis, quote attributed.

70 Lyrics by Redd Evans and John Jacob Loeb, posted at: wikipedia.org/wiki/Rosie_the_Riveter.

71 Bossidy and Charan, 19.

72 Tom Landry, 1924–2000: head coach of the Dallas Cowboys 1960–1988, winner of two Super Bowls; quote attributed.

73 Henry Ford, 1863–1947: founder of Ford Motor Company; quote attributed.

74 Marcus Buckingham and Curt Coffman, *First, Break All the Rules* (New York: Simon & Schuster, 1999), 111.

75 President Theodore Roosevelt, 1858–1919: twenty-sixth president of the US; quote attributed.

76 T. S. Eliot, *The Sacred Wood*, (first published in 1920; currently, West Valley City, UT: Walking Lion Press, 2011).

77 Aristotle, 384–322 BC: Greek philosopher and author; quote attributed.

78 Theodore Roosevelt, quote attributed.

[79] President Theodore Roosevelt, "Citizenship in a Republic," speech at the Sorbonne, Paris, April 23, 1910, posted at: theodoreroosevelt.com.

[80] Laurence J. Peter, 1919–1988: US educator and writer, best known for *The Peter Principle* (1969); quote attributed.

[81] Abraham Lincoln, 1809–1865: sixteenth president of the US, quote attributed.

[82] From *War Games*, a 1983 MGM movie written by Lawrence Lasker and Walter F. Parkes, directed by John Badham.

[83] Posted at: www.huffingtonpost.com/grant-cardone/kill-the-competition_b_495589.html.

[84] Mike Krzyzewski, *Leading with the Heart* (New York: Business Plus, 2000), 121.

[85] Laches, cited in Plato, *Courage*, Benjamin Jowett, trans., posted at: classics.mit.edu/Plato/laches.html.

[86] Newt Gingrich and William R. Forstchen, *To Try Men's Souls* (New York: Thomas Dunne Books, 2009).

[87] Dr. Martin Luther King Jr., speech on April 3, 1968, Memphis, TN.

[88] Billy Graham, "A Time for Moral Courage," *Reader's Digest*, July 1964.

[89] Sun Tzu, *The Art of War*, Lionel Giles, trans., posted at: classics.mit.edu/Tzu/artwar.html.

[90] De Pree, 11.

[91] Tzu, classics.mit.edu/Tzu/artwar.html.

[92] "CEO Disease," Bloomberg/*Businessweek*, March 31, 1991, posted at: businessweek.com/stories/1991-03-31/ceo-disease.

[93] Dane Miller, sited in *Great by Choice*, Jim Collins and Morten T. Hansen (Harper Collins, New York, 2011).

[94] "CEO Disease."

[95] Ibid.

[96] Ibid.

[97] Rick Warren, *The Purpose Driven Life* (Grand Rapids: Zondervan, 2002), 17.

[98] Peter Drucker, 1909–2005: author of thirty-nine books on management theory and practices, recipient of numerous awards and honors; quote attributed.

[99] Posted at: www.businessweek.com/stories/2005-11-27/the-man-who-invented-management.

[100] Posted at: www.leadershipnow.com/druckerremembered.html.

[101] Max De Pree, *Leadership Jazz* (New York: Dell Publishing, 1992), 131.

[102] Ross Perot, 1930–: US businessman and presidential candidate 1992 and 1996; quote attributed.

[103] Billy Graham, 1918–: American Christian evangelist and spiritual advisor to presidents; quote attributed.

[104] Neville Chamberlain, 1869–1940, British politician and prime minister 1937–1940; quote from wikipedia.org/wiki/Neville_chamberlain.

[105] Bill Clinton, 1946–: forty-second president of the US, speech at the Campus Progress National Student Conference, July 13, 2005.

[106] Will Rogers, 1875–1939: American humorist and actor; quote attributed.

[107] Edward R. Murrow, 1908–1965: American radio and television journalist, testimony before a Congressional Committee, May 1963 (wikiquote.org/wiki/Edward_R._Murrow).

[108] Thomas Lanier "Tennessee" Williams, *Camino Real* (New York: W. W. Norton & Co., originally published in 1953).

[109] Chuck Swindoll, 1934–: American evangelical pastor, author, educator; quote attributed.

[110] General Colin Powell, *18 Lessons for Leaders*, posted at http://www.1000advices.com/guru/leadership_18lessons_cp.html.

[111] David Lloyd George, 1863–1945: prime minister of Great Britain during World War I; quote attributed.

[112] Indra Nooyi, 1955–: CEO of PepsiCo; quote attributed.

[113] http://en.wikipedia.org/wiki/Paul_harvey.

[114] Lencioni, 200.

[115] Walter Isaacson, *Steve Jobs* (New York: Simon & Schuster, 2011), 567.

[116] This phrase has been used by many people (e.g., Steve Jobs, Peter Drucker, Colonel Sanders, and Ray McKinley).

[117] Posted at: www.interstatebatteries.com.

[118] Posted at: www.truetcathy.com.

[119] S. Truett Cathy, *Eat Mor Chikin—Inspire More People* (Decatur, GA: Looking Glass Books, 2002), 124.

[120] Posted at: www.amazon.com/Anthony-Rossi-Christian-Entrepreneur-Tropicana/dp/0830849998/ref=sr_1_1?s=books&ie=UTF8&qid=13453 35169&sr=1-1&keywords=anthony+rossi.

[121] Posted at: www.washingtonpost.com/blogs/the-buzz/post/the-faith-of-joe-gibbs/2011/10/06/gIQAxehpQL_blog.htmlgameplanforlife.com.

[122] Posted at: http://en.wikipedia.org/wiki/Henry_parsons_crowell.

[123] Posted at: www.marykaytribute.com/HerLife.aspx.

[124] Posted at: www.amazon.com/Its-Easier-Succeed-Than-Fail/dp/0840790309/ref=sr_1_5?s=books&ie=UTF8&qid=1345336258 &sr=1-5&keywords=truett+cathy.

[125] Lee Strobel, *The Case for Christ* (Grand Rapids: Zondervan, 1998), 13.

⁑ ⁑ ⁑ ⁑

ABOUT THE AUTHOR

Raised with farmers, small shop owners and blue collar workers in Oklahoma and north Georgia, Dick entered the business world after receiving a BS in Aerospace Engineering from Georgia Tech: "My first hard lesson was learning that I am not a very good engineer."

After five years in engineering, a move to the project and marketing side of the business launched a successful career that was highlighted by serving five years as president, and then CEO, of a $300M/2000 employee aerospace company with facilities in three states. A two-year stint as president of a large commercial shipyard was followed by serving for six years as the executive pastor of his home church in Franklin, Tennessee.

Dick re-entered the business world by launching his leadership development company, Hard Lessons, in 2009: "Hard Lessons is not the story of a superstar leader featured in Forbes or on CNBC. Though I have enjoyed a large measure of success, Hard Lessons is as much about failure as success. Much of what I have learned, I have learned the hard way. Hard Lessons is my leadership journey openly shared—the good, the bad, and the ugly."

In addition to Hard Lessons, speaking, and writing, Dick serves on the boards of Brightstone (special needs adults) and Williamson College. *16 Stones* is his first book.

Dick—married for 45 years to his partner in life, Dottie—is the proud father of two daughters, Elizabeth and Cathy, and the grandfather of three rowdy and loud buddies: Aaron, Caleb and Seth. Franklin, Tennessee has been his home for most of the last 30 years.

For information about Hard Lessons, go to www.hard-lessons.com.

CPSIA information can be obtained at www.ICGtesting.com
Printed in the USA
LVOW11s1027221113

362239LV00005B/6/P